BRITISH TAXATION AND THE COMMON MARKET

BRITISH TAXATION AND THE COMMON MARKET

A volume of essays

DOUGLAS DOSSER

with contributions by

JOHN DODSWORTH
THEODOR GEORGAKOPOULOS
KLAUS SCHNEIDER

CHARLES KNIGHT & CO. LTD.
LONDON
1973

Charles Knight & Co. Ltd
11/12 Bury Street, London EC3A 5AP
Dowgate Works, Douglas Road, Tonbridge, Kent

First published 1973

ISBN 0 85314 200 9

Printed and bound in England by
STAPLES PRINTERS LIMITED
at The Stanhope Press, Rochester, Kent.

Contents

Foreword

THE research programme at the University of York which has produced this and other published studies in the field of tax harmonization has continued through a period when British interest in the subject has transformed itself from the meagre to the very intense. Even during the period leading up to British entry, the White Papers of February 1970 and July 1971 made virtually no mention of the tax consequences of British accession. By 1973 however, the situation is radically changed, with the introduction of the VAT on Community lines, the imminent action on excise duties, the impending conflict between British intentions and the Commission's plans for a Community corporation tax, and the development desired by Britain of a Community regional and industrial budgetary expenditure programme.

The state of flux in fiscal matters produced by British entry makes publication of research results, with the inevitable delays in publication, particularly problematic and prone to the criticism of 'out-of-dateness'. No doubt, some of the hypotheses used in this volume will prove to have lost their current usefulness when they appear. This is unavoidable in any Common Market policy study at present, especially in the case of the VAT, although it can always be counter-argued that, in such a fast-changing field, the supposed dead hypothesis, e.g. the economic effects of a high-rate VAT system, can be re-vivified by a new turn of events a year or so hence.

So much for the problem of timing. This volume has issued from the research programme in Public Sector Studies at the University of York, supported by a programme research grant in Public Sector Studies made to the Department of Economics and the Institute of Social and Economic Research in the

University of York by the Social Science Research Council. It is a continuing programme, and in that part of it devoted to fiscal aspects of UK entry into the European Community, studies of the economic consequences of new developments in tax harmonization will already be under way when this volume appears.

The contributors to this volume have either held full-time research posts in the Institute financed by SSRC funds, or participating members in the Public Sector Studies Programme Research Group. The work has benefited by the general evaluation of that group, and by the special and greatly valued help over a long period always generously given by Professor Alan Peacock, head of the Department of Economics, and Professor Jack Wiseman, director of the Institute of Social and Economic Research.

My own contributions were completed at PEP, London, who have kindly provided a base for my research work during a sabbatical year's leave from the University of York.

Douglas Dosser
28 February 1973

Contributors

Douglas Dosser is Professor of Economic Theory at the University of York and director of the EEC section of the Public Sector Studies Programme at York.

Theodore Georgakopoulos completed his doctoral degree at York and is now Professor of Public Finance at the University of Athens.

John Dodsworth is Research Fellow on the Public Sector Studies Programme at York.

Klaus Schneider was previously Research Fellow on the Public Sector Studies Programme at York and is now an official of the Commission of the European Communities.

1

Introduction to the Theory and Practice of Tax Harmonization

by Douglas Dosser

'TAX HARMONIZATION' in this volume applies specifically to tax coordination among nations in process of integration in a customs union or economic union. It is thus distinguished from 'tax reform' which a country may undertake on its own account, or as part of a new world-wide fashion in taxation—the discussion of a VAT for the USA is in this category.

Another alternative, 'tax union', has been used. This is particularly apt when new taxation arrangements are made rather as an adjunct to customs union. But tax harmonization is the subject of this volume.

Tax harmonization is a new topic, stemming from the Treaty of Rome in 1958, and more or less confined to the development of the European Economic Community. Though mainly related to European conditions, some parts of the discussion, especially in the theoretical sections, have implications for other economic groupings, such as the Central American Common Market, East African Economic Union, etc.[1].

Tax harmonization in this volume, of course, is looked at entirely from the EEC viewpoint, but to include those nations which have just become members in 1973.

The theme of the discussion of the course of tax harmonization over the last 15 years can be policy-oriented—the twists and turns of EEC (and latterly, British) philosophy and policy proposals—or it can be theoretical—the attempt to develop principles or a framework against which to evaluate alternative

[1] More specifically for developing countries see D. Dosser, 'Customs Unions, Tax Unions, Development Unions', in *Modern Fiscal Issues* (ed. R. Bird & J. Head), University of Toronto Press, 1973.

future policies. Both themes are intermingled in this chapter.

Taxes in the Community, 1958

The variety of taxes in the six founding members at the time of the signing of the Treaty of Rome in 1958 was very great. Among general sales taxes, though value-added tax systems existed, 'cascade' systems or taxation of gross values at each stage of production were equally important. They formed the German system, for example, and single-stage taxes at the retail stage comprised the Italian system.

Similar variety existed among excise duties. The sheer number varied immensely from little more than the classical five (manufactured tobacco goods, hydrocarbon oils, wine, beer and spirits) in the 'northern' countries to a bewildering variety, including coffee, sugar, salt, matches, etc., in Italy. Further, the method by which the State took its share of revenue from excisable goods varied from state-controlled manufacturing at one extreme, e.g. tobacco goods in France and Italy, to fiscal imports based on value, weight, strength, quality, etc., at the other.

In the case of the corporation tax, this did not even exist as a separate tax form in some countries, e.g. Italy. In other countries, it was either quite separate from the personal income tax, with a single or a split-rate (differing on distributed and undistributed profits), or partially integrated with the personal income tax system so that part of corporation tax paid on distributed profits could be credited against a shareholder's income tax liability.

The personal income tax system itself was differentiated in very many respects among the Six, not just as regards rates and allowances but also administrative procedures, compliance and enforcement.

Finally, the variety in the para-tax system involved in social security was profound. The balance between sickness, industrial injury, unemployment, and pensions was markedly different, and the methods of financing these benefits even more so.

Little would be gained from stating the 1958 situation in greater detail[2]. The great point to be made is how diversified

---

[2] For additional detail, see D. Dosser and S. S. Han, *Taxes in the EEC and Britain: The Problem of Harmonisation*, International Institute of International Affairs/PEP, 1968.

the tax systems of the Six were. During the period covered by this chapter, 1958–73[3], harmonization has been imposed on this diversity as part of Community policy. The central questions are: how much has been achieved, what have been the principles underlying such achievements, and do these principles stand up to analysis?

In approaching these questions, a little problem arises over the identification of harmonization. A Community Directive is clear-cut, whereas policy at the Proposal stage will probably but not definitely be adopted, and Commission Working Group Reports even less certainly. A further complication is that community policies, even after Directives, may be more or less vigorously applied in particular Member States. But on the other hand a positive factor is to be found in 'spontaneous harmonization' where Member States, particularly new or aspirant members, may anticipate Community policy in tax changes they make. Recognizing these shades of meaning attaching to tax harmonization, we shall mention most such developments in this chapter, but in later chapters, where hypotheses have to be used, they are best based on the firmer ground of Directives and Proposals.

Tax Harmonization Policy, 1958–73

The Treaty itself, surprisingly in view of its emphasis on unification, impinged rather lightly on the rich tax diversity noted in the previous section.

As is well known, there is a clear demand for the harmonization of indirect taxes in Article 99 of the Treaty, but without any specification of what is meant by harmonization. The position is even more vague in the case of direct taxes. Article 100 says that laws should be approximated in these respects: no further details are given.

Thus the development of tax harmonization policy of the Community has come entirely from the process of study by Committees or Working Parties (sometimes composed of outside experts, sometimes of officials of the Commission), informal discussion with Member States of committee suggestions, drawing up by the Commission of a Proposal to the

[3] Subsequent chapters look forward also, of course, and chapters 6 and 7 specifically deal with the transition period of enlargement, 1973–78.

Council of Ministers, which may become a Directive, binding on Member States.

This process first got under way with general sales taxes, but then not until 1963 with the report of the Neumark Committee.

It was this Committee which recommended the value-added form of general sales tax. The dominant reason was its superiority over the then current 'cascade' system in Germany, which distorted industrial structure, since tax payments could be reduced by vertical integration. Subsequently, the VAT has replaced many other sales tax systems, e.g. single-stage systems at the wholesale and retail stages, where other justifications, if any exist, are needed.

The Neumark Committee, besides recommending the *structure* of a Community sales tax, committed itself also to the basic *jurisdictional principle* for internationally-traded goods. This was to be the so-called restricted origin principle, whereby goods crossing borders within the Community were to carry the tax of the country of production (the origin principle), whilst goods coming from outside the Community were to bear the tax of the country of consumption (the destination principle). It will be seen that such a system entails an equalized Community rate of tax if undesired distortions in purchasing patterns and Member State revenue receipts are not to occur.

Harmonization of the general sales tax was off to a flying start with the Neumark Report in 1963, but in subsequent years, realization of its recommendations has been slow and piecemeal. In the period 11 April 1969 to 9 December 1969, six Directives were issued, whose net effect was to set up the VAT *structure*. No progress has been made on the equalization of rates (nor hence on the establishment of the restricted origin principle). Indeed, developments as regards rates have gone in a reverse direction with the accession of new members with VAT rates outside the established range of the Six.

Accession of new members has even meant an increase in the number of exceptions to the homogeneous structure, particularly the exclusion of foodstuffs from the UK VAT.

Looked at from one angle, progress on the VAT appears slow, but, on the other hand, the transformation of one of the most important taxes in several States with complex fiscal structures has been achieved in just a few years.

The only other Commission activity in the field of tax harmonization lies at the Working Party-Proposal stage in the corporation tax and excise duties.

Historically, the next tax dealt with by a Commission committee was the corporation tax, but progress has been held up since then, and no Proposals or Directives have been issued[4].

The recommendations for a Community corporation tax structure came in the van den Tempel Report of 1969. This came out in favour of an entirely separate, single-rated, corporation tax with no integration with the personal income tax as would exist with a credit system[5]. This came at a time when such a system was not favoured in most of the Six, and, in the case of the UK, a little before she planned to abandon that very system. Consequently, progress has been stymied, with the Commission facing the dilemma whether to make a Proposal of a system favoured by itself but out of favour in most Member States.

Excises, with all their complications, have been the subject of internal discussion in the Commission for a long time (there has not been an outside committee in this case), and at long last a Proposal has been published. The principal element of this is that only the five traditional excises will be harmonized. The details of how this is to be done are discussed in the chapter on excises. We may note that the general theme of VAT harmonization prevails: structural uniformity first, with the aim of rate equalization later.

There is virtually nothing to report on the final two great areas of the fiscal system, social security and the personal income tax. There is some intention to harmonize some parts of member-state social security systems but, other than a few regulations about the rights of migrant workers, no action. And there is no intention of harmonizing the personal income tax in the foreseeable future.

Only three harmonizable fields, VAT, excises and the corporation tax, are the subject of more intensive study in other chapters of this book.

A problem remains with the other two that, although neither

---

[4] Except for two Directives on relatively minor technical matters.

[5] The reasoning behind the Tempel recommendation will, of course, be dealt with more fully in chapter 4.

the Commission nor this volume treats them as harmonizable, they may nevertheless be affected indirectly in the medium term, or directly in the long run. Indirectly, revenue implications of harmonization in the three primary fields may require consequential changes here, and especially as the idea of a 50/50 split between indirect/direct tax revenues has been mooted as a target. And in the long run, they may have to be acted on directly if factor mobility does extend from capital to labour. This will be touched on again in the theoretical discussion which follows, though in the short and medium term to which this book relates, it is the three harmonizable fields of taxation which will claim our detailed attention.

The Purposes of Tax Harmonization

We have had an indication of the attempts to harmonize taxes in the three harmonizable fields. It is for these, specifically, that the question needs to be asked: what is the purpose of harmonization?

In the Treaty of Rome and in the Neumark Report the explicit reasons given for harmonizing these taxes derive from such sentiments as 'free competition', 'removing obstacles to trade', etc. This is what may be called the *ideological* approach, as opposed to the *analytical* approach.

The ideological sentiments do, of course, have a groundwork in economic theory. They follow from making an analogy between the removal of tariffs as hindrances to economic welfare, and the removal of tax differences as similar hindrances. The analogy is partly false.

In the case of the tariffs, the ideological approach and the analytical approach partly converge; unimpeded trade makes the most of different countries' comparative advantages, and maximizes output available from given resources. The main exception concerns less-developed countries, where economic welfare may for a time be maximized if the gains from industrialization achieved through protection are thought to outweigh losses due to the disruption of free trade.

But in the taxation case, the divergence of the ideological approach and the analytical approach is both wider and deeper. It is wider because divergences apply to developed countries as well as to less-developed countries. It is deeper because the functions of an important tax are so much greater than a tariff. The function of a tariff is mainly protective, and even its revenue aspect is not very important in developed countries. But in the case of a tax, its functions cover revenue raising (and therefore the provision of government services), income-redistribution, macro-stabilization, etc.

Consequently, when the question of harmonizing or co-ordinating a major tax in several different countries in a common market is discussed, it surely ought not to be treated in the same ideological way as were tariffs, using the general concepts of free competition and free trade. Rather, each case must be analysed, taking account of the whole apparatus of modern public finance—not only allocative aspects, but revenue, income-distribution, stabilization and growth as well.

In a previous work[6], the author has tried to make a start at developing a general theory for the evaluation of tax harmonization, covering the different parts of public finance mentioned above. Leaving aside the detail in that work, perhaps the most important theme was the development of what was called the *differentials* approach. The ideological approach cited above leads rather naturally to what one termed the *equalization* approach.

The differentials approach implies a full analysis of the effects of any proposed tax harmonization measure in all of the areas of public finance listed earlier. It is recognized as inevitable that a particular measure will appear as beneficial to some economic objectives, injurious to others. It was suggested that a weighting system was needed to balance these gains and losses, and to decide if a particular tax harmonization measure was conducive to economic welfare overall. These weights were political rather than economic. It follows that a particular tax harmonization policy may appear beneficial overall, even if the usual comparative advantage trade effects (those that underlie the assumed benefits of free competition) are negative. Conversely, a case may appear where there are positive trade or allocative effects, but these are outweighed by adverse stabilization effects.

---

[6] 'Economic Analysis of Tax Harmonization', chapter 1 of *Fiscal Harmonization in Common Markets*, ed. C. S. Shoup, Columbia University Press, 1966.

It also followed from the general theory that a tax harmonization move which did appear desirable might be analogous to the tariff case, in that tax differentials were to be eliminated. But equally, the most desirable tax harmonization move might be quite different from the tariff case, and involve the setting of specific differentials between the Member States or between regions in the Common Market. This would tend to occur when the benefits under stabilization, growth, etc., from a particular set of differentials outweighed the assumed losses from not having unimpeded trade or unimpeded factor movements.

The general analytical approach is simply a matter of judging all feasible tax harmonization policies by this multi-dimensional economic welfare function, and proceeding with those which show up the best. Equalization or the tariff-equivalent case is only one of this possible set.

In order to implement this system of analysis, it is necessary to be able to judge the effects of different tax harmonization policies on the major fiscal objectives listed, i.e. allocation, stabilization and growth. It is also necessary to have analyses of the revenue and income distribution effects.

All of these involve separate or specific theories. When they are all knit together to evaluate a particular tax harmonization policy, using the idea of a welfare function or objective function, this is what might be called the general theory of tax harmonization. This, of course, is where detailed progress is to be made. But before we turn to them, there are some general problems which relate more to the general theory.

The Main Problems of Harmonization

We will deal with five important problems. Only the first was discussed in my earlier exposé of the general theory[7].

(i) Conflict of Interest

When a tax harmonization policy is discussed there are many interests involved. At the highest level, there is the entity of the Common Market, then there are the nation states, and there is the outside world. It has not been made clear whose welfare function is in use to judge the desirability of any particular

[7] 'Economic Analysis of Tax Harmonization', op. cit.

policy. It was recognized that weights would be necessary to balance the different economic effects, and that those weights were political. Now the various entities will weight different effects differently; for example, the Commission may value overall stabilization of the European economy far more highly than one particular state which is in reasonable balance between inflation and unemployment. Or, a nation with several backward areas might favour fiscal arrangements encouraging growth more than the Community.

There is no answer to this conflict of interest except a political one. The areas of economic analysis and politics can be fairly well marked off. Economics should give information of the effects of particular fiscal arrangements on particular economic objectives. Politics weights them within a political entity, and the political process decides between competing political entities.

(ii) Total versus Partial Tax Harmonization

It is implied in the earlier part of this paper, and indeed also in our earlier work[8], that each tax harmonization policy, whether it referred to sales taxation or corporate taxation or part of these two systems, could be evaluated independently according to the system outlined. This was to assume the legitimacy of partial as opposed to general equilibrium. But it is now quite clear that two policies analysed jointly will not add up to the effects of each analysed separately. It is a relevant question whether any particular policy is being introduced in isolation, or in association with certain others, or in association with complete tax harmonization in some sense. A policy which might appear desirable on its own, later becomes undesirable when further tax harmonization measures are undertaken.

There is no simple answer to this problem. General equilibrium can be defined: it is the total effects of that part of the fiscal system which will eventually be harmonized—sales taxes and excises and corporate taxation. But the time span of this total harmonization plan is very long. And answers are required for specific and piecemeal tax harmonization policies. The only resort is to assume that partial analyses are proxies to changing

[8] 'Economic Analysis of Tax Harmonization', op. cit.

a part of the whole system in the *final* general equilibrium frame, whereas the specific policy is actually being initiated in the initial general equilibrium frame. If amendments to the results for the change through time of the general equilibrium frame can be noted, this is some consolation.

(iii) Product Mobility and Factor Mobility

Customs union theory proceeds in a world of factor immobility, though newer work on tariffs and trade gets out of this framework. By having to consider tax unions involving corporate tax and capital movements we have perforce to move into the shifting sands of a factor-mobile world, and incidence in such a world.

But it is not satisfactory even to consider sales tax union in only a factor-immobile model, a corporate tax union in a factor-movement model.

Some rate calculations concerning general sales tax shift the burden to factors, whilst calculations for corporate tax would, on some recent hypotheses on shifting, pass some of the burden on to consumer prices.

Hence, strictly speaking, there are trade changes in the factor-immobility model arising from changes in product prices and relative factor prices (which may change comparative advantages). And in the second model, allowing factor movement, these may stem from shifted-back sales taxes as well as the tax on the factor, the corporate income tax.

Thus, as an ideal, we should work in two settings, the customary customs union setting of factor immobility and the setting where differences in factor endowments are changed by movements of capital. Both sales taxes and corporation tax need consideration in each setting.

But again it has to be admitted that most work in tax harmonization, including subsequent chapters of this book, will still be confined to the factor-immobile world of customs union theory and tariff-reduction trade calculations, or will not make the above two-model distribution at all clearly.

(iv) Neutrality Effects versus Welfare Effects

In an earlier work[9], all the economic effects which should be

[9] 'Economic Analysis of Tax Harmonization', op. cit.

taken into account in the objective function: revenue and income-distribution effects, as well as allocation, stabilization and growth effects, were lumped together. This is probably not quite legitimate. If one thinks of what might be the real economic benefits of tax harmonization, these cannot be said to be changes in tax revenue or alterations in income distribution. For these can be effected by the nation alone by changes in its own tax system. What is more to the point is whether new fiscal arrangements can be made, in a common market, which leave the size of the revenue and the state of income distribution in a Member State intact (assuming it has already attained a preferred position in these respects), but add to short-run real national income or long-term stability or growth compared with the non-harmonized situation. If we may assume that these are desirable prospects for a Member State, if obtainable without changes in revenue or income distribution, they are in a sense 'costless'. It does not seem fair to count in as benefits to a tax harmonization policy consequences which may in fact stem from changes in revenues or distribution and which may therefore have been achieved by the nation state acting on its own.

Therefore the real economic benefits of tax harmonization should be judged in a situation of ceteris paribus as regards revenue and income distribution; this is what determines the 'neutrality' of a tax harmonization policy.

In order to judge whether a tax harmonization policy is being analysed in a neutral situation, it is clear that it is just as necessary to consider its revenue and income distribution effects, as it is to consider its allocative, stabilization and growth effects.

(*v*) *Proxies for the Variables in the Welfare Function*

In the general theoretical approach, the objectives of improved allocative efficiency, stabilization, and growth are broadly and vaguely stated. As soon as implementation of the theory begins, especially statistical work, a closer specification of something measurable is required. This measurable proxy may not correspond completely with the grand objective in the general welfare function.

a. Allocative Efficiency. In tariff work, increases in trade arising from tariff reductions are taken to indicate improvements in specialization, and hence global allocative efficiency. Whilst we at present use the same proxy for the harmonization policies, the correspondence is not very satisfactory. For it can be shown that pre-harmonization tax differentials are 'forcing' trade to take place which would not do so in a 'free-trade' environment, so that a reduction in trade may indicate an increase in welfare.

b. Stabilization. We first distinguish external and internal stabilization. But we also have to distinguish whether we mean that a tax harmonization policy actually improves a disequilibrium *situation*, or improves the *mechanism* for dealing with it. For external stabilization, there is an actual benefit if the deficit is reduced, though care is necessary in specifying which parts of the account—current visibles, current invisibles, capital—we are referring to. The mechanism may be altered in various ways: a change in propensities to import and in import elasticities, or in the range of policy weapons to deal with a deficit.

Internal stabilization may be thought of in a number of ways—inflation or unemployment may be altered, or the structural relationship between them can be shifted, or the policy weapons enhanced or limited.

c. Growth. It may not be so much overall growth that is considered, but its regional deviations. In either case the distinctions between growth from increased inputs and from various sources of productivity improvement may be used, though many sub-proxies will be necessary.

In the case of 'neutrality' effects, revenue and income distribution, these can be measured directly.

It is clear from the preceding that the object of particular economic and statistical studies in tax harmonization is to evaluate a policy's effect on trade, balance of payments, etc.

But the policy itself needs a little more elaboration. Unlike the tariff case, where a rate change is the obvious policy move, in the tax field, practice has shown that the harmonization of a particular tax proceeds in stages. Three should be distinguished: *structural change; change in jurisdictional principle;* and *rate change*. At any one time there may be under discussion a tax harmonization policy involving either one, or more than one conjointly, of these stages.

We are now in a position to lay out the nature of a 'special study'. Given a particular tax, it involves ascertaining the effects of one of the economic variables in the right-hand column of a policy instrument on the left.

Change of:	*Economic variables:*
Structure	Revenue
	Income distribution
	Trade
Jurisdictional principle	Balance of payments
	Inflation/unemployment
Rate	Productivity or regional growth

Thus, if we were dealing with the sales tax, a special study might evaluate the effects of the change-over from 'cascade' to 'value-added' (structural change) on revenue or on trade. In the case of corporation tax, the effects of a uniform 15 per cent withholding on internationally-transmitted earnings on balance of payments may be the subject of a special study.

All of these potential special studies, besides being linked by the general welfare function, are knit together by a common procedure, which is, in fact, essentially the same as that used in tariff and customs union work, but with the manifold extensions we have added for the tax case. The step-by-step procedure is:

a. Statement of initial position before harmonization;
b. The change (structural, jurisdictional, rate) proposed by the harmonization programme;
c. Effects on the economic variables under study.

It is more than obvious that the analytical methods just suggested have never before been brought to bear on the tax harmonization policy of the Community. This has been rather simpliste, based on *uniformizing* the taxes as regards structure, jurisdictional principle and rates, rationalized by certain *ideological* sentiments.

The Advent of Economic and Monetary Union

Economic and monetary union, as a goal of the Community, was publically introduced by the Werner Report in 1969, endorsed at the Hague Summit, 1969 and by the Paris Summit, 1972. These events radically change the outlook for tax harmonization, theory and policy. Up to 1969, and probably one could say, up to January 1973 we had the old conflict described in the previous section, between an *actual policy* of uniformization, which stemmed from sentiments about free trade, distortions of competition, and proposals for new tax structures, equalized or differentiated, which were based on an analysis as to what was economically most advantageous in each case.

The inauguration of economic and monetary union has broken the bonds of the old ideology, and necessarily brings to the fore such issues as economic management and planning, by the Commission itself or by Member States acting in consultation with each other.

Therefore, a more analytical approach is bound to be ushered in. Curiously, however, the new situation gives a new impetus to both the role of fiscal unification and fiscal differentiation (or, as it is now better to call it, fiscal flexibility).

Fiscal unification is given a new rationale (compared with the old ideological basis of undistorted competition) by economic and monetary union in this way. If at least some functions of economic management in the union are to be conducted by the Commission itself (it already conducts agricultural policy management, of course) it requires substantial resources of its own for the European Budget.

A crucial step was taken to provide this, also at the Hague Summit of December 1969, in agreeing that from 1975, the Six would render up to a 1 per cent VAT yield to the Commission, in addition to the yield of each country's common external tariff and agricultural levies on extra-Community imports. The details and implications of this system are fully dealt with in chapter 5.

Now, such a system, replacing direct contributions based on Member State national incomes, is only viable and equitable if the basis or structure of the tax, in this case the VAT, is uniform in each Member State.

Thus, one implication of economic and monetary union, the necessity for a growing European budget, is the need, on the grounds of functional economic management, for a unification of structures of VAT and other taxes so used, and on equalization of at least the Community segment of that tax.

On the other hand, economic and monetary union clearly

re-inforces the requirement of substantial fiscal flexibility. For monetary union implies the extinction of exchange-rate policy, national money-supply policy and rate-of-interest policy (as capital markets integrate). Thus all the pressure is put on fiscal and budgetary weapons, for short-term stabilization (usually taxes) and long-term structural re-adjustments (usually national/regional tax-and-expenditure policies).

Consequently, there is an imperative functional demand for fiscal differentiation by Member States or regions. This may apply to rates only (with uniformized tax structures) or differentiated structures.

A Reassessment in the Light of Economic and Monetary Union

Economic and monetary union has overtaken the commencement of the studies of alternative harmonization policies discussed above.

We really need to think of a two-tier fiscal system, comprising the Community system and that of each Member State[10].

Whilst inter-Member State equity demands a uniformization of *structures* of the Community taxes, there remains the question of determining differentials, both as regards the rates of the Community taxes and the Member State taxes, from considerations of economic objectives.

The only prior, and additional, question is: which taxes most appropriately form the Community tax system? Equity only demands structural uniformity of such a tax; consideration of economic efficiency will help determine whether it be the VAT, corporation taxes, or some other tax system.

This issue is not determined as yet, and is only discussed in this volume under 'future policy'. It is a substantive issue of chapter 7. The studies of each of the harmonizable fields in succeeding chapters to this are non-committal as to whether they are analysing some of the effects of an element of the Community tax systems or of Member State taxes whose revenues will remain with them. The analysis of some of the economic effects is derived in either case, without at present exploring the issue of its level in the two tier system.

---

[10] More accurately, a three tier system to include local finance, but regional/local authority budgets have not been included in the present volume.

Special Studies in this Volume

An implementation of the analytical schemes of some of the above sections (pages 6 and 15) for the effects on the British fiscal system of British entry into EEC would be impossibly ambitious at present. Difficulties arise at each of the three stages:

(i) Provision of comparative information on structures and rates of tax in Britain and EEC is itself an enormous undertaking.

(ii) Harmonization measures themselves are in dispute or in the early formative stage in EEC; also they may be modified on enlargement of the Community. Further, the division between Community taxes and resources, and Member States, is a wide-open question.

(iii) Considerable new theoretical, as well as statistical, work is required for the evaluation of some tax harmonization changes on some of the economic variables listed.

Let us first enlarge on these difficulties, and then be more positive and state what it is hoped this volume can achieve.

The prior stage of the statement of the initial comparative position of taxes in EEC and Britain is mainly a problem of scale, though several methodological issues also have to be settled.

(i) As regards indirect taxes, the statement of the initial position in a group of industrial countries should be laid out as follows:

a. Tax Structure. This will show a mixture of general sales taxes, taxing at different stages and in different ways (though by 1973, this complex structure will be much simplified as we have seen), and of excises of many different kinds.

b. Jurisdictional Principle. This is the simplest aspect to state. Internationally-traded products may be taxed on the origin or destination principle or, in a group of countries, both principles may prevail.

c. Rates. This is the most important and the most difficult part of the pre-tax union statement. We have the difficulty of nominal rates *versus* some form of effective rates *versus* some form of incident rates. By nominal rates, we mean those which appear in legislation. Effective rates try to get to the fiscal charge on the economic unit after various *non-market* factors are allowed for (e.g. allowances, compliance with the law, special loopholes, etc.). Incident rates aim at the real loss-of-income or burden on an economic unit after shifting[11].

In tariff work, concentration has been put on unweighted and weighted 'nominal' tariffs, and more recently on deriving 'effective' tariffs or rates of protection. There has been little attention paid to incidence.

The relation between the concepts and calculations on the tax side and tariff side is as follows. Nominal tax rates are equivalent to unweighted nominal tariffs. Effective tax rates correspond to weighted (by import values) nominal tariff rates. The only incident rates in tariff work consist of the assumption that part of the price change of European exports due to a tariff change is not passed forward.

The 'effective' rates of Grubel and Johnson[12], derived from input-output data, do not yet have an equivalent in tax harmonization work. It is true that Grubel and Johnson included indirect taxes in their calculations. But they consolidated sales and excise taxes and also, by obscuring tax structures and jurisdictional principle, make it difficult to use the data to assess changes implied by current EEC tax harmonization, which apply to *sales* taxes and mainly to structure.

Aggregate figures for an earlier year have been calculated in nominal, effective and incident form for Britain and the EEC[13].

Turning from indirect taxes to corporate taxation, there is a similar situation: a wide international difference in structure, jurisdictional principles, and rates.

In the aggregate, the situation is easier as regards structure, for the EEC countries all have a corporation tax similar to USA and UK, separate from the personal income tax.

But the problems of jurisdiction principle are more compli-

---

[11] These distinctions were developed and are elaborated upon in D. Dosser, 'Fiscal and Social Security Barriers to Economic Integration in the Atlantic Area', chapter VIII of *Studies in Trade Liberalisation*, ed. B. Balassa, Johns Hopkins Press, 1967.

[12] 'Nominal Tariffs, Indirect Taxes, and Effective Rates of Protection: The Common Market Countries 1959', *Economic Journal*, December 1967.

[13] D. Dosser and S. S. Han, op. cit.

cated in the corporate tax case than in indirect taxation. There is a similar duality of possible principle: taxation in country of source of earnings, taxation in country of residence of the owner of capital.

There is no general agreement as to which principle is to be applied; agreements (tax treaties) to modify the inherent double taxation of capital income crossing an international frontier vary greatly and the initial situation is very haphazard.

Thus there is no need to express the insignificant initial structural differences, and it is pointless to lay out the tax treaty arrangements, which is more a lawyers' job. So the *effect* of the complete, partial or zero modification of the inherent double taxation by tax treaty is built straight into the rate tables.

Tables of aggregate nominal, effective and incident rates all have to be in matrix form to show the different *net* rate payable according to the pair of countries between which the capital income is flowing, and even which way!

There is one further problem to add to the misery. The net tax rate differs in law according to the type of establishment which a company may be operating abroad and the degree to which profits are remitted home.

Tables are available to show the nominal and effective aggregate rates of corporate tax in Britain and EEC taking these complications into account[14]. Incident rates have not been attempted in view of the continuing and unresolved controversy as to the degree of forward shifting of the corporate tax.

(ii) Turning to the intermediate stage of analysis. the actual or hypothetical tax harmonization changes to be assumed, the agenda of actual or possible changes in the initial situation is fairly straightforward in the tariff case. It may be the formation of a customs union like the EEC, with a common external tariff, or of a free trade area like EFTA, where sovereignty over third-party tariffs remains. Or a percentage across-the-board cut in tariffs between trading blocs, as in the case of the Kennedy Round. Each of these may provide the starting point of the analysis.

---

[14] In Dosser and Han, op. cit.

But in the tax case, it will already be clear that we have to contend with many further difficulties. The change in the tax situation produced by the formation of the Common Market or economic union, as stated earlier, may be one of (a) structural coordination; (b) change in jurisdictional principle; or (c) rate harmonization. And in the early stages, the evidence of EEC, in respect of both indirect and direct taxation, is that (a) and (b) precede (c).

The agenda of actual and not-unfeasible changes requiring a qualitative or a statistical analysis can be very great. We shall try in this volume to keep to the practical measures which have been taken, or which appear likely, in the EEC itself.

(iii) The final stage of the analytical approach is, of course, the ascertainment of the effects, expressed qualitatively or statistically, of a particular tax harmonization measure on revenue, income distribution, allocative efficiency (or trade), stabilization and growth.

Progress here must ultimately be of the greatest importance. But for the present it is the most difficult. Not only on account of the weight and difficulty of statistical work, but because there are many theoretical difficulties (such as those outlined earlier as theoretical problems of the general theory of tax harmonization) which await solution, and which will be resolved by work which would be more appropriate in the learned journals than in the practical volume it is hoped this will prove to be.

But it is not such a great loss that great progress cannot yet be made in this final stage. For we shall find that there would be no basis in the case of most taxes, in expected tax harmonization policies, to move to such a stage at present.

The feature of this volume that must be emphasized is that in practice the accent is currently on different stages in the case of different taxes, and the chapter on each tax reflects this.

Thus the chapters are inevitably not symmetrical: some will properly put the emphasis on the possible, but still hypothetical, shape of future tax harmonization; elsewhere, an attempt might be made to establish the effects of a known tax harmonization proposal.

In the chapters which follow, the different aspects of the tax situation are considered in the manner indicated overleaf:

	Initial Structure, Rates, etc.	*Tax Harmonization Policies*	*Economic Effect*
Sales Taxes	Surveyed	Known	Revenue, Income Distribution, Trade, Balance of Payments
Excises	Surveyed	Conjectured	Revenue, Income, Distribution.
Corporation Tax	Surveyed	Conjectured	—
Social Security	Surveyed	Conjectured	—

'Conjectures' may be strong (Community decisions imminent) or weak, and this affects the confidence with which one can proceed to a study of economic effects.

Whilst the progress that can be made in each chapter study is thus disparate, the whole knits together in a common theory and common procedure, as outlined earlier in this introduction.

The final chapter, ideally, should re-orient the economic effects from a tax-by-tax basis to an effect-by-effect basis, and make the distinction between Community taxes and effects and harmonized Member State taxes and effects. As will be evident, this is not really possible at present, since only effects of a few tax harmonization measures can be confidently evaluated, and the division between the Community public finance system and that of Member States is unknown.

This is the first volume of its kind, implementing in practical detail and statistics the theory of tax harmonization which has been developing over the last few years. It is an on-going venture: more areas of the map can be filled in as new tax harmonization proposals, and the degree and timing to which Britain has to implement them on entry into the EEC become known.

2

The Value-Added Tax

by T. Georgakopoulos

Introduction

The value-added tax (VAT) has already been introduced by a number of countries in Europe, in others the tax is in the process of its introduction, while certain other countries are considering its pros and cons before taking a final decision. The recent wide acceptance of the tax by an ever-increasing number of countries is mainly due to the fact that the EEC has decided to use this form of sales tax as the common system of turnover tax. The EEC choice of VAT is mainly based on the fact that the tax has been shown to have a number of advantages over the traditional forms of sales taxes (cascade turnover, single stage, etc.) in a common market[1]. Moreover, the tax itself has certain advantages over other forms of sales taxes and consequently some countries are considering its introduction irrespective of the question of membership of the EEC.

Britain has already announced the introduction of the VAT as a substitute for the purchase tax (PT) and the selective employment tax (SET)[2]. Since the tax has been rejected in the past[3], the recent change in attitude towards this tax in Britain should be mostly attributed to the country's decision to join the Common Market. Yet, it is shown below that the VAT will probably cause some beneficial effects, especially on the balance of payments, in the UK.

In this chapter, we shall briefly discuss the proposed VAT system in the UK and compare it with the corresponding VAT

---

[1] See especially, International Bureau of Fiscal Documentation, *The EEC Reports on Tax Harmonisation. The Report of the Fiscal and Financial Committee*, Amsterdam 1963, henceforth cited 'The Neumark Report'.

[2] See 'Value-Added Tax', Cmnd 4929, HMSO, London, 1972.

[3] See *Report of the Committee on Turnover Taxation*, HMSO, London, 1964, and *The NEDO Report*, HMSO, London, 1969.

systems in the Common Market. A short account of some of the possible effects of VAT substitution in the UK will then be considered.

Some Background Knowledge about VAT

Definition and Forms of VAT

The value-added tax is a form of sales tax which taxes only the value added by firms at the various stages of production and distribution. The tax can apply to one or a limited number of stages, but, as it comes to be adopted in Europe today, it tends to be a general tax levied at all stages of production and distribution, including the retail stage.

On the basis of the tax treatment of capital goods, the VAT can take one of the following three forms[4]:

(i) The consumption-type VAT, which allows deduction of all purchases of the capital goods by firms on a current basis. The tax is, in this case, confined to consumption goods only and, under certain conditions, it is equivalent to a retail sales tax levied on consumer goods[5].

(ii) The income-type VAT, which allows deduction of capital depreciation only and not of the whole value of capital goods at the time they are purchased; and

(iii) The product-type VAT, which does not allow for any deduction of capital goods on either current or depreciation basis.

Out of the three forms of VAT the first seems to be generally adopted by nearly all countries which have introduced or are about to introduce the tax. This variety of VAT has a number of advantages over the other forms of VAT, the most important of these being that it provides a stimulus for investment.

Methods of computation

There are two alternative methods for the calculation of VAT.

(i) The direct or 'accounts' method, under which the firm's value-added is computed first and the tax rate is then applied

---

[4] See Clara Sullivan, *The Tax on Value-Added*, Columbia University Press, 1965.

[5] See C. S. Shoup, 'Consumption Tax, and Wages Type and Consumption Type of Value-Added Tax', *National Tax Journal*, June 1968, pp. 153–61.

thereto. On the basis of whether value-added is computed by addition of the various components of the value-added, i.e. wages, profits, etc., or by subtracting the firm's purchases from its sales, two varieties of the direct method are distinguished: the direct additive and two direct subtractive methods.

(ii) The indirect or invoice method, under which the firm's value-added is never known but the tax liability is calculated indirectly. In this method, the tax liability is computed by applying the tax rate to total sales and subtracting the tax paid on purchases. This method, known as the 'tax credit' method, is widely regarded as the best and is used by all European countries that have adopted the value-added tax. Its advantages are[6]: (a) it is simple, both for the firm to operate and the tax authorities to audit; (b) it provides a cross-check among firms, because the tax paid by the selling firm appears as a deduction to the buying firm; (c) it avoids all problems concerned with the direct computation of a firm's value-added; and (d) it facilitates the handling of rate differentiation and exemptions. This last advantage is of particular importance in a customs union using the destination principle of taxation. For it makes possible the equalization of the tax burden on domestic production and imports, thereby making the VAT neutral from the point of view of its impact on trade.

Arguments for the VAT

The VAT possesses a number of important advantages. Some of them are advantages of the value-added principle, and are therefore present under any form of VAT, while others are present only in the case of certain forms of VAT, and especially of the consumption type.

The most important advantage of VAT is perhaps its economic neutrality. This is an advantage of the VAT itself, and is held by all forms of VAT. Thus, because the tax is levied only on the value which is added by each firm, and not on the firm's total turnover, the total tax burden levied on a product is independent of the number of stages through which the product passes (this was not the case with the cascade turnover taxes).

[6] See John Due, *Indirect Taxation in Developing Economies: The Role and Structure of Customs Duties, Excises and Sales Taxes*, Johns Hopkins Press, 1970.

As a result the VAT does not lead to vertical integration of firms for the sole purpose of tax avoidance. Nor is there any reason for firms to change the location of particular functions along the line of production and distribution, provided all sectors, including retailing, are covered by the tax. On the contrary, if VAT extends only up to the wholesale stage, it then encourages firms to push activities to the retail stage and has consequently the same distorting effects as a wholesale tax.

A second advantage of VAT is its neutrality with respect to trade. This advantage is however present mainly in the case of the consumption-type VAT, because only this type of VAT treats domestic production and imports of consumer goods truly alike, and does not result in substitution between domestic production and imports. Moreover, only the consumption-type of VAT is fully rebated on exports and does not therefore affect the price of the country's exports abroad. On the other hand, the forms of value-added tax that fall also on capital goods are not truly neutral with respect to trade because the component of the VAT accumulated into the value of capital goods may, if market conditions allow it, be shifted on to the price of final products, through capital depreciation. As a result, imports of final products will bear the VAT at the nominal rate, but domestic production will also bear the component of the VAT allocated to investment expenditure and later reflected in higher prices of final products produced domestically. Similarly, exports of final products are rebated for the direct component of VAT only, while no tax rebate is granted for the indirect component falling on exports through investment.

Another important advantage of VAT is the built-in cross-check feature, which can reduce tax evasion considerably. Thus, the tax which is paid by the selling firm is reported by the buying firm as a credit against its tax liability. The buyer does not have any benefit to buy from the seller tax free because it will have less tax to credit and consequently its own tax liability will be higher. This advantage is not clearly an advantage of the VAT per se, but of the particular method used for the computation of the VAT, i.e. .the tax credit method'. However, it is the nature of the tax that allows the use of this method, which is clearly inapplicable in the case of other forms of sales taxes; and although many devices can be used against tax evasion, in the case of such taxes, the tax credit method seems to provide an important advance in this respect.

Finally, the VAT can become a truly consumption tax, which has admitted advantages over the other forms of sales taxes. These other taxes are more difficult to impose on consumers' expenditure alone, and do tend to overlap on to investment.

Problems and Limitations

To set against the above advantages, the VAT has a number of limitations. Some of them are again due to the nature of the tax as a form of sales tax, whilst others are the result of either the particular method employed, or the coverage of the tax.

The main disadvantage of the VAT per se is its greater complexity. The concept of the tax is more difficult to understand than other forms of sales taxes, and its administration requires well organized book-keeping. This makes the VAT a less advantageous tax for less developed countries where book-keeping is not very advanced.

Another important drawback of the tax, which is not a drawback of the VAT itself, but of the broadness of the tax base which is necessary if VAT is going to be a truly general tax and function satisfactorily, is the greater number of registered firms with which tax authorities have to deal. In Britain, for example, the number of firms that will fall into the VAT system and will have to file returns is estimated to amount to about 2 million as compared with 65,000 firms that were taxed under the purchase tax[7].

A third problem is the necessity of avoiding or minimizing exemptions and rate differentiation, otherwise the tax becomes extremely complex and loses certain of the above-mentioned economic advantages. Exemptions create difficult problems, especially when they are granted to intermediate stages before the final one[8]. Rate differentiation also creates administrative problems and deprives the tax of some of its economic advantages[9].

---

[7] See John F. Due, *Indirect Taxation in Developing Countries*, op. cit., p. 131.

[8] See Alan A. Tait, *Value-Added Tax*, McGraw-Hill, New York, 1972. See also W. Missorten, 'Some Problems in implementing a Tax on Value-Added', *National Tax Journal*, December 1968.

[9] See Clara Sullivan, *Value-Added Tax*, op. cit.

Finally, the VAT meets serious problems when applied to certain sectors, especially to services such as banking, insurance, etc.[10].

VAT Systems in the Common Market

The Commission's proposals concerning the VAT

The value-added tax has been first recommended by the Neumark Committee as the common turnover tax to be introduced by the six EEC countries[11]. In a series of Directives, the Commission later provided the Member States with more information concerning the details about the tax. The first Directive informed the Member States that they had to replace their systems of turnover tax by a common system of tax on value-added, the broad lines of which were determined in the Directive[12].

The second Directive provided more details about the common VAT to be introduced[13]. The following are the main elements of the proposed VAT system:

(i) The tax should be a general one, applying to all stages of production and distribution, including the retail stage. Until the abolition of fiscal frontiers with respect to intra-community trade, however, the Member States are given the option to restrict the application of the proposed VAT only up to and including the wholesale trade stage and, where appropriate, apply an independent compensatory tax on the retail stage.

(ii) The tax to be levied on the deliveries of goods and the rendering of services within the country as well as importation of goods. Taxation of services is compulsory only when services affect the price of goods. A list of these services is given. Member States are free to tax or not all other services not included in the list. These are mainly services rendered to the final consumers, such as services supplied by doctors, hospitals, hairdressers, etc. Banking services have also been left out of the list.

(iii) The tax is to be restricted only to consumer goods, the

[10] See Alan A. Tait, *Value-Added Tax*, op. cit., pp. 20–41.
[11] See the Neumark Report, pp. 145–149.
[12] For details see *European Taxation*, November–December 1968, Appendix pp. 299–309.
[13] Ibid.

tax paid with respect to purchases of investment goods being creditable.

(iv) The base of the tax must include all costs and taxes other than the value-added tax itself. In the case of imported goods the value for customs purposes, increased by all duties, taxes and levies which are due by reason of importation, with the exemption of the VAT itself, constitutes the taxable base.

(v) Until the abolition of fiscal frontiers, the Member States are free to determine tax rates and exemptions independently, within broad limits set in the Directive. A normal rate applicable to as wide a range of goods as possible has been postulated, but increased or reduced rates have been allowed to apply in certain cases. Imports should be taxed at the same rates with domestic production of similar products. However, after the abolition of the fiscal frontiers common rates and exemptions will have to be introduced by all Member States. This common long-run VAT system will be the object of an expected future directive.

(vi) Deliveries of goods outside the territory of a state as well as the rendering of services relating to such goods, or to goods in transit, must be excluded from the tax. The destination principle is therefore effectively recommended.

(vii) The Member States are given the option to apply to small enterprises, for which subjection to the normal system of VAT might encounter difficulties, the particular system best adapted to their national requirements and opportunities. The same option is also granted with respect to those engaged in agricultural activities, until common methods for the application of VAT to transactions relating to agricultural activities are submitted by the Commission and approved by the Council.

A third Directive laid down the main provisions for the extension of VAT to agriculture[14], while a fourth Directive contains some important measures towards an approximation of the VAT systems in the Common Market countries[15] (abolition of fiscal frontiers by 1 January 1974, bringing retail transactions into the scope of VAT, reduction of the number of rates, etc.).

---

[14] See Council of the EEC: Proposed third Directive, Terms and Conditions for the Common Application of the Tax on Value-Added to Operations Related to Agricultural Products, Brussels, February 1968.

[15] See *European Taxation*, Vol. 9, November 1969.

VAT systems adopted in the Common Market

Following the general principles laid down in the above Directives, five of the six EEC countries substituted the VAT for their pre-existing turnover taxes, while France has extended the scope of its existing VAT to conform to the Commission's proposals. The following are the main features of the newly introduced VAT system[16]:

(i) *Coverage of the taxes.* All the VAT systems introduced by the common market countries are general, that is, levied at all stages of production and distribution including the retail stage. However, a number of exemptions have been made and cases of zero-rating are recognized in all countries.

(ii) *Form of VAT.* All VAT systems are of the consumption type, i.e. they all allow for a deduction of capital expenditure on a current basis.

(iii) *Method of computation.* All systems use the credit method for the computation of the tax. The tax rate is applied to the total value of sales, but a credit is recognized for tax paid on the firms' purchases.

(iv) *The tax base.* The value added to products destined for consumption purposes within a firm constitutes the taxable base. Imports duties, excise taxes, as well as any other taxes incorporated into the sales value of a product are also included into taxable base. The value-added tax itself is, however, excluded from the taxable base. Imports also are exposed to the tax, while exports are zero-rated.

(v) *Tax rates and exemptions.* Value-added tax is levied at

Table 1. Effective rates of the VAT in the Common Market (1 January 1972)

Country	Lowest	Intermediate	Normal	Luxury
Belgium	6.0	14.00	18.00	25.00
France	7.5	17.65	23.45	33.33
Germany	5.5	—	11.00	—
Italy (proposed)	6.0	—	12.00	18.00
Luxembourg	5.0	—	8.00	—
Netherlands	0.0	4.00	14.00	—

[16] For more details see *European Taxation*, Vol. 8, November–December 1968 and Vol. 10, August 1970. See also International Bureau of Fiscal Documentation, *Value-Added Taxation in Europe*, Guide to European Taxation, Vol. IV.

different rates in each country within the Six. Table 1 shows the rates presently in force in the EEC countries.

There is also a wide divergence between the member countries as regards exemptions. The main exemptions are banking and insurance services, as well as certain other services mainly provided to final consumers such as services rendered by lawyers, doctors, hospitals, etc. Special measures have also been taken in all countries with regard to small traders[17].

Turnover Taxes in the UK

The main turnover tax operating in the UK since 1940 has been the purchase tax (PT)[18]. It is a single stage tax, levied at the wholesale stage on certain goods used for domestic consumption. The tax is levied on these goods even when they are used in industry or commerce. The range of goods on which the tax falls is fairly narrow compared with the base of any other turnover tax in Europe. Moreover, the rates at which the tax is levied on the various groups of products differ widely. Consequently, one can look at the tax as either a single turnover tax or a number of excises.

The base of the tax is the price which the goods would fetch on a sale from a wholesaler to an independent retailer buying in ordinary quantities. Charges for delivery and packing are also included in the taxable base but the tax itself is excluded.

The tax was applied at four different rates previous to the 1971 reduction: $13\frac{1}{4}$ per cent for clothing, footwear, furniture, domestic hardware, etc.; 22 per cent for confectionery, soft drinks and ice cream; $36\frac{2}{3}$ per cent for certain articles of domestic use; and 55 per cent for luxury goods, such as furs, jewellery, clocks and watches of precious metals, etc. In July 1971 these rates were reduced by $\frac{2}{11}$. The reduction was, according to the Chancellor's statement, a first step towards the complete abolition of the PT, with effect from 31 March 1973, when the VAT is introduced[19].

The PT brings in a considerable proportion of the total tax

[17] For details see International Bureau of Fiscal Documentation, *Value-Added Taxation*, op. cit.

[18] For details see John F. Due, *Sales Taxation*, Routledge and Kegan Paul, 1957, pp. 202–234. See also the *Annual Reports of the Commissioners of Her Majesty's Customs and Excise*.

[19] See the Chancellor's speech in Hansard, 21 March 1972.

revenues. Table 2 below shows the evolution of the revenues from this tax over the last ten years. In 1970, just before the reduction in the tax rates, the tax brought in nearly one-fifth of the revenues raised through indirect taxes and 7.2 per cent of the total tax revenues.

Table 2. The revenues from the PT over the period 1960–1970 (£mn)

Year	Revenues from the PT	Revenues from all taxes on expenditure	Total central government tax revenues*	Ratio (1):(2)	Ratio (1):(3)
	(1)	(2)	(3)	(4)	(5)
1960	510	2,620	6,813	19.5	7.5
1965	647	3,758	10,156	17.2	6.4
1968	971	5,391	14,188	18.0	6.8
1970	1,291	6,636	17,984	19.4	7.2

* including National Insurance Funds

Source: National Income and Expenditure 1971, table 38, p. 44.

Of a peculiar nature is the Selective Employment Tax (SET). The tax was announced in the Budget of May 1966 and put into force in September 1966[20]. Although administratively similar to a payroll tax, the scope of its introduction seems to call for a treatment as a supplement to the PT. For one of the main arguments for its introduction was that the service sector was relatively lightly taxed as compared with manufactured products, which were exposed to excise taxes and the PT. The SET was partly intended, therefore, to improve the structure of indirect taxes in the UK, by redressing the balance between services and manufacturing. Its introduction on a per capita, rather than an ad valorem or unit of product, basis was intended to discourage the use of labour in the taxed sectors, thereby making more of it available for the expansion of the manufacturing sector.

The tax was levied at four different rates and applied to employees in the construction and distributive trades and most service industries. Employers in manufacturing had the tax refunded, with the refund being higher than the actual amount of tax, thereby serving as a subsidy. Both the structure and the rates of the tax have changed over time. Of special interest

[20] See HM Treasury, *Selective Employment Tax*, Cmnd 2986, 1966.

Group of Expenditure	Expenditure in 1970 in (£mn)	At 1970 rates: Tax yield in (£mn) PT	SET	Total	Effective rates (%) PT	SET	Total	At 1972 rates: Tax yield (£mn) PT plus SET	Effective rates (%) PT plus SET
I. Consumers' Expenditure	31,257	1,116.0	312.0	1,428.0	3.57	1.00	4.57	947	3.03
1. Food	6,363	125.9	65.9	194.8	1.98	1.04	3.02	144	2.26
2. Drink	2,178	7.7	10.0	17.7	0.35	0.46	0.81	14	0.64
3. Tobacco	1,720	3.2	14.2	12.4	0.19	0.83	1.02	16	0.93
4. Housing	3,904	12.3	21.7	34.0	0.31	0.56	0.87	19	0.49
5. Fuel and light	1,489	3.1	5.7	8.8	0.21	0.38	0.59	2	0.13
6. Clothing and footwear	2,634	202.0	30.2	234.2	7.67	1.15	8.82	182	6.91
7. Motor cars and motor cycles	980	184.6	7.0	191.6	18.83	0.71	19.54	120	12.24
8. Furniture and floor coverings	626	70.1	7.1	77.2	11.19	1.13	12.32	60	9.58
9. Radio and other electrical	661	126.1	6.0	132.1	19.08	0.91	19.99	81	12.25
10. Other household goods	910	55.7	10.2	65.9	6.12	1.12	7.24	48	5.27
11. Books, newspapers, etc.	463	1.0	4.8	5.8	0.22	1.04	1.26	4	0.86
12. Chemists' goods	455	95.7	6.4	102.1	21.03	1.41	22.44	61	13.41
13. Miscellaneous recreational goods	718	83.3	3.4	86.7	11.60	0.47	12.07	50	6.96
14. Other miscellaneous goods	381	93.6	7.1	100.7	24.57	1.86	26.43	64	16.80
15. Running costs of motor vehicles	1,679	1.8	19.3	21.1	0.11	1.15	1.26	11	0.66
16. Travel	1,025	2.0	3.7	5.7	0.19	0.36	0.55	1	0.10
17. Communication services	319	0.6	1.2	1.8	0.19	0.37	0.56	—	—
18. Entertainment	566	22.1	17.0	39.1	3.91	3.00	6.91	19	3.36
19. Other services	4,186	25.2	71.1	96.3	0.60	1.70	2.30	51	1.22
II. Investment Expenditure	8,886	139.0	134.0	273.0	1.56	1.51	3.07	167	1.88
III. Public Authorities' Expenditure	9,055	31.0	352.0	383.0	0.34	3.89	4.23	171	1.89
IV. Exports	11,182	16.0	46.0	62.0	0.14	0.41	0.55	49	0.44
Total:	60,380	1,302.0	844.0	2,146.0	2.16	1.39	3.55	1,334	3.21

Sources: Blue Book 1971, Central Statistical Office, author's estimates.

for the purposes of this study is the recent reduction of the rates by 50 per cent, the reduction of which is the result of the government's decision to abolish the SET and substitute it by the VAT.

Neither the PT nor the SET are strictly confined to consumers' expenditure, they also strike at other categories of expenditure. Columns 2–7 of table 3 present the allocation of the revenues from the two taxes among the various forms of final demand and the main groups of consumers' expenditure in 1970, before any tax reduction took place, while columns 8–9 present the allocation of the tax revenues from the two taxes at 1972 tax rates.

The PT falls heavily on only a small number of commodity groups, while others are effectively exempt. The category 'other miscellaneous goods' is charged at the highest effective rate. Chemists' goods are taxed at slightly lower rates, while the categories 'radio and other electrical' goods and 'motor cars and motor cycles' fall in a third class. The categories 'miscellaneous recreational goods', 'furniture and floor coverings', 'clothing and footwear', and 'other household goods' are also taxed at fairly high rates though not as high as the other groups.

The SET, on the other hand, fell somewhat evenly on the various consumer goods and services. This was mainly the result of the large exemptions from the SET granted within the service sector, as well as of the fact that most services, especially the ones that are provided by the distributive trades sector, enter the cost of the various commodities in the production of which these services are used. It is doubtful, therefore, whether the tax did, as intended, restore the fiscal balance between goods and services, or whether it was simply an additional tax falling more evenly on the consumption of both goods and services.

The UK Value-Added Tax

The VAT has just been adopted in the UK. Its introduction was announced nearly two years ago and a Green Paper[21] was then published setting out some general proposals about the VAT. A year later a White Paper[22] followed, containing more

[21] See Cmnd 4621, HMSO, 1971.
[22] See Cmnd 4929, HMSO, 1972.

detail about the structure of the tax, the probable tax rates, etc. The basic rate of 10 per cent was confirmed in the 1973 budget. The following are the main features of the VAT in the UK[23].

The tax is levied at all stages of production and distribution, including the retail stage. It is, however, restricted to consumers' expenditure, with full credit being granted for the tax falling on investment expenditure. Government expenditure is for the most part not brought under the scope of the VAT. Finally, exports are zero rated[24]. Like all systems in the Common Market, therefore, the proposed VAT for the UK is of the consumption type.

The base of the tax is the value added to consumer goods and services in the UK as well as the value of imports. Customs duties, excise taxes and all other charges, with the exemption of the value-added tax itself, are included in the taxable base. However, not all consumers' expenditure is brought under the scope of the tax. Contrary to the provisions of the EEC Directives and to the actual VAT systems adopted by the Common Market countries, the British VAT provides for a wide range of consumers' expenditure to be zero-rated, while at the same time a large number of exemptions is recognized.

The main zero-rated consumer goods and services are: most food, water supply, books, newspapers and magazines, fuels, construction of building, public transport and prescribed drugs and medicines.

The main exemptions from the tax are those small traders with an annual turnover of less than £5,000. This exemption will take about half a million traders out of the tax. However, an option has been given for those traders who wish to subject themselves voluntarily to the tax to do so. Other large areas of exemptions are: land, insurance, postal services, betting, gaming and lotteries, finance, education and health.

The tax will be applied at the same rate on all goods and services subject to the VAT. The standard rate proposed by the Chancellor is 10 per cent. Moreover, the standard rate can be

---

[23] For more details see HMSO, *Value-Added Tax*, op. cit. See also R. S. Nock and M. A. Pickering, 'The Shape of the Value-Added Tax', *British Tax Review*, March–April 1972.

[24] It is only a small part of VAT that falls on exports of certain services where rebating is impossible.

subjected to a 20 per cent regulator. Besides, a separate 10 per cent surcharge is to be levied on new and imported cars at the wholesale level.

Table 4 below presents the amount of revenues that the VAT will bring in under alternative nominal tax rates[24a]. As shown in the table, both the 7½ per cent and the 10 per cent rates will bring in less revenues than the PT and the SET at the 1970 tax rates. If VAT is going to bring in the same revenues as the two taxes which are to be abolished, a tax rate of about 12½ per cent must be adopted. However, a large part of the PT and the SET had been falling on government expenditure, while the corresponding amount of VAT that falls on government expenditure is comparatively much smaller. If we leave out the amount of tax allocated to government expenditure as representing transfer of money from one pocket of the government to the other, then a 10 per cent rate of VAT will bring in the same amount of revenues as those taxes which are to be abolished.

On the other hand, if a comparison is made with the revenues under the 1972 rates of the PT and the SET then a 7½ per cent rate of VAT will bring in the same yield as the PT and the SET. The 10 per cent rate which is proposed by the Chancellor brings in much more revenue than the PT and the SET at the 1972 rates. In fact, the revenues that will be raised under the 10 per cent rate of VAT will be higher than the revenues that the PT and the SET would bring in, even if tobacco and drinks are left out of the VAT.

Effects of VAT Substitution in the UK

The substitution of the VAT for the PT and the SET in the UK will affect the British economy in a number of ways: prices, income distribution, the balance of payments, stabilization and growth will all be affected. In this chapter we shall concentrate on the price, income distributional and balance of payments effects.

[24a] The statistical analyses were completed before the confirmation of a basic rate of 10 per cent, and a reduction of excises to leave the total tax on excisable products roughly the same, were announced in the 1973 budget, as this volume went to press. The alternative assumptions here may well become relevant again, as rate changes are required for future EEC tax harmonization.

Table 4. The yield of the VAT in the UK under alternative nominal rates

Group of Expenditure	Tax yield in £ million				Effective Rates (%)			
	7½%	10%	12½%	15%	7½%	10%	12½%	15%
I. Consumers' Expenditure	1,188	1,584	1,980	2,381	3.80	5.07	6.33	7.62
1. Food	61	81	101	122	0.96	1.27	1.59	1.92
2. Drink	162	216	270	324	7.44	9.92	12.40	14.88
3. Tobacco	127	169	211	254	7.38	9.82	12.27	14.77
4. Housing	53	71	89	107	1.36	1.82	2.28	2.74
5. Fuel and Light	—	—	—	—	—	—	—	—
6. Clothing and footwear	180	240	300	360	6.83	9.11	11.39	13.67
7. Motor cars and motor cycles	115[a]	153[a]	191[a]	230[a]	11.73	15.61	19.50	23.47
8. Furniture and floor coverings	41	55	69	83	6.55	8.78	11.02	13.26
9. Radio and other electrical goods	40	54	68	81	6.05	8.17	10.29	12.25
10. Other household goods	64	85	106	128	7.03	9.34	11.65	14.06
11. Books, newspapers, etc.	—	—	—	—	—	—	—	—
12. Chemists' goods	26	35	44	53	5.71	7.69	9.67	11.65
13. Miscellaneous recreational goods	48	64	80	96	6.68	8.91	11.14	13.37
14. Other miscellaneous goods	21	28	35	42	5.51	7.35	9.19	11.02
15. Running costs of motor vehicles	34	45	56	68	2.02	2.68	3.33	4.05
16. Travel	—	—	—	—	—	—	—	—
17. Communication services	16	21	26	32	5.01	6.58	8.15	10.03
18. Entertainment	32	43	54	65	5.65	7.60	9.54	11.48
19. Other services	168	224	280	336	4.01	5.35	6.09	8.03
II Investment Expenditure	110	147	184	220	1.24	1.65	2.07	2.47
III. Public Authorities' Current Expenditure	44	58	73	87	0.48	0.64	0.81	0.96
IV. Exports	8	10	13	15	0.07	0.09	0.12	0.13
Total:	1,350	1,799	2,250	2,700	2.24	2.98	3.73	4.48

Sources: National Institute Economic Review, May 1972, tables 10 and 12: author's estimates.

[a] including the 10% surcharge announced by the Chancellor.

Price effects

The proposed VAT substitution will affect both the level and the structure of product prices in the UK since, as shown above, the VAT falls on the various products at effective rates different from those at which the PT and the SET fell. The size of the price changes depends upon the degree of forward shifting of both the taxes to be abolished and the VAT, which is to be introduced. The VAT is usually assumed to be fully shifted on to product prices. The broadness of the tax as well as the administrative procedure employed for the collection of the VAT tend to support the hypothesis of a 100 per cent forward shifting. The assumption of complete forward shifting however is not satisfactory in the case of the PT and perhaps more so in the case of the SET. The problem becomes more complicated and uncertain because of the probable lack of symmetry in tax shifting. For even if the PT and the SET are shifted forward on to prices, their abolition may not necessarily lead to price reductions to the same extent. We shall therefore employ four alternative assumptions of tax shifting: (i) all taxes are fully shifted on to prices; (ii) VAT and PT are fully shifted, but only 40 per cent of SET is shifted; (iii) VAT is fully shifted while only half of PT and SET is shifted; and (iv) VAT is fully shifted but the PT and the SET are not. Those four assumptions will probably provide us with the most likely range of the price changes expected to result from the introduction of the VAT in the UK.

Table 5 gives the changes in the over-all consumer price level which will probably result from the introduction of the VAT at alternative nominal rates[25]. The price changes with reference to the 1970 tax rates as well as the ones with reference to the 1972 tax rates are presented in turn. Two alternative situations are considered: (i) the situation where the VAT falls on the excised products, drink and tobacco, at the standard rate; and (ii) the situation where the excised products are zero-rated. As shown in the table, the over-all consumer price level will fall if a $7\frac{1}{2}$ rate is adopted provided the two taxes are fully shifted on to prices or the PT is fully shifted while the SET is

[25] The formal model through which these estimates have been derived is presented in T. Georgakopoulos, 'Trade Effects of Tax Substitution: The Value-Added Tax in the U.K.' (forthcoming).

Table 5. Effects of VAT substitution on consumer prices, under alternative shifting assumptions of the PT and the SET

Shifting hypothesis	Change in consumer price index, 1970 tax rates								Change in consumer price index, 1972 tax rates							
	7½%		10%		12½%		15%		7½%		10%		12½%		15%	
	I	II	I	II	I	II	I	II	I	II	I	II	I	II	I	II
1. 100% for both the PT and the SET	−0.8	−1.7	0.5	−0.7	1.9	0.2	3.3	1.2	0.8	−0.2	2.2	0.8	3.5	1.8	5.0	2.9
2. 100% for PT, 40% for SET	−0.2	−1.2	1.2	−0.1	2.5	0.9	3.9	1.9	0.9	0.1	2.6	1.1	4.1	2.4	5.8	3.9
3. 50% for both PT and SET	1.6	0.6	2.9	1.6	4.3	2.7	5.8	3.7	2.4	1.4	3.8	2.4	5.2	3.5	6.6	4.5
4. Both taxes unshifted	4.0	3.0	5.3	4.0	6.8	5.0	8.3	6.1	4.0	3.0	5.3	4.0	6.8	5.0	8.3	6.1

Source: Tables 3 and 4.

Notes: Alternative I presents the price changes with no reduction in excise taxes, while alternative II presents the price changes when excises are reduced to such an extent as to leave the tax burden on excised products the same as before.

shifted only by 40 per cent. If a 10 per cent rate is adopted, the price level will fall only if excised products are zero-rated. In all other situations prices will go up compared to prices under the 1970 tax rates for the PT and the SET. The price increases can be very high especially if the two taxes are not fully shifted on to prices and a high rate of VAT is adopted. Thus, if a 10 per cent VAT is adopted and the abolition of neither the PT nor the SET is reflected in lower prices, the consumer price index will increase by more than 5 per cent provided drink and tobacco are also exposed to the VAT. If these excised products are zero-rated, prices will increase by 4 per cent. More substantial price increases will take place if a 12½ per cent or a 15 per cent rate is adopted and the abolition of the PT and of the SET is not reflected in lower prices (zero-shifting). The over-all consumer price level will increase more if a comparison is made with the situation under the 1972 rates of the PT and the SET. As shown in columns 9–16 of table 5, the VAT will in this case most probably lead to price increases no matter what tax rate will be adopted.

Table 6, on the other hand, gives the change in the structure of consumer prices resulting from the 10 per cent VAT substitution[26]. As shown in this table, prices of other miscellaneous goods will fall substantially compared with the corresponding prices under the PT and the SET at the 1970 tax rates. Prices of 'chemists' goods' and of 'radio and other electrical goods' will also fall but not to the same extent as the prices of the first category. The price of food, 'motor cars and motor cycles', 'furniture and floor coverings', 'miscellaneous recreational goods' and clothing will also fall slightly, while prices of all other categories will rise. The price reductions are smaller and the price increases higher when a comparison is made with the situation under the 1972 tax rates of the PT and the SET. If different VAT rates are adopted the absolute changes in the prices of the various categories will clearly change, but the relative price changes, which are of importance for our later analysis and especially for the estimation of the trade changes to follow the structural change in consumers' expenditure, will remain the same. Similarly, the size of the absolute price

[26] For their derivation see, T. Georgakopoulos, 'Trade Effects of Tax Substitution'.

Table 6. Absolute and relative price changes of consumer goods and services consequent upon the introduction of a 10% VAT in the UK*

Groups of Consumers' Expenditure	1970 tax rates		1972 tax rates	
	absolute price change	relative price change	absolute price change	relative price change
1. Food	−1.8	−2.3	−1.0	−2.9
2. Drink	10.1	9.5	10.3	8.0
3. Tobacco	10.1	9.5	9.9	7.6
4. Housing	1.0	0.4	1.4	0.8
5. Fuel and light	—	—	—	—
6. Clothing and footwear	0.2	−0.3	2.4	0.3
7. Motor cars and motor cycles	−4.7	−5.2	4.0	1.8
8. Furniture and floor covering	−3.9	−4.6	−0.9	−3.0
9. Radio and other electrical goods	−12.9	−13.3	−4.4	−6.5
10. Other household goods	2.3	1.8	4.5	2.3
11. Books, newspapers, etc.	—	—	—	—
12. Chemists' goods	−16.1	−16.4	−6.2	−8.2
13. Miscellaneous recreational goods	−3.5	−4.0	2.1	0.0
14. Other miscellaneous goods	−20.6	−21.0	−10.2	−12.1
15. Running costs of motor vehicles	1.5	0.9	2.1	0.0
16. Travel	—	—	—	—
17. Communication services	6.4	5.9	—	—
18. Entertainment	0.8	0.2	4.6	2.4
19. Other services	3.2	2.7	4.4	2.2
20. Consumers' expenditure abroad	—	−0.5	—	−2.2
Total Consumers' Expenditure	0.5	—	2.2	—

Sources: Tables 3 and 4.

* As percentage of the price inclusive of tax.

changes of the various categories of consumers' expenditure will be different, if different shifting hypotheses are employed. The relative price changes will remain unaffected by the degree of forward shifting, provided the shifting coefficient is the same for all categories of consumers' expenditure.

Redistributional effects

Provided the value-added tax falls on the various groups of consumers' expenditure at rates different from those at which the PT and the SET fell, the tax substitution will most probably affect income distribution in the UK. With the proposed structure of the VAT, however, the redistributory effects will not in fact be very important, since the VAT exempts food as well as certain other groups of consumer goods and services not taxed under the PT. The redistributory effect will clearly be different depending on whether excised products are taxed or not. We shall therefore consider the redistributory effects of the VAT substitution both in the situation where excised products are brought under the scope of the VAT and in the case where they are zero-rated. The exercise will however be restricted to equal yielding situations ('differential incidence' in the Musgravian terminology)[27].

Previous works on the measurement of the redistributory effects of either the budget as a whole or certain items of it, have discussed a number of both methodological and statistical problems present in the exercise[28]. Some of these problems are also present in our investigation and a short discussion of the most important of them seems warranted.

First, a proper income concept to be used in the investigation should be chosen. Should one use national income, personal income, or any other aggregate? Should one use the pre-tax substitution, the after-tax substitution or any other intermediate income concept? The choice of the income concept is very important since statistical results have been shown to be quite sensitive to the concept of income employed. Statistical considerations have imposed upon us the use of gross income, as given in the Family Expenditure Survey[29]. However, since we are here concerned with differential incidence, the over-all picture of the redistributory effects of VAT substitution will not change substantially if any other income concept had been employed.

[27] See R. A. Musgrave, *The Theory of Public Finance*, McGraw-Hill, 1959, pp. 227–230.

[28] See R. A. Musgrave, 'Estimating the Distribution of the Tax Burden', in *Income and Wealth Series X*, Bowes and Bowes, London 1964. See also J. L. Nicholson, 'Redistribution of Income in the U.K. in 1959, 1957 and 1953', in *Income and Wealth Series X*, and A. T. Peacock, *Some Problems in the Measurement of the Redistributory Effects of the Government Budget*, Istanbul, 1968.

[29] See *Family Expenditure Survey*, Report for 1971, HMSO.

Second, a proper income unit must be chosen. Individual income earners or families can alternatively be used. The choice between the two mainly depends upon the purpose of the investigation. If one is interested in measuring redistribution for social purposes, the family seems to be a more appropriate unit. On the other hand, if interest is focussed on the economic effects of income redistribution, the individual income earner may be a more appropriate unit. In this study, the family will be used as the relevant unit, mainly because the available information on consumers' expenditure in the Family Expenditure Reports is in terms of the family as a whole and not the individual earners.

Third, the allocation of the tax burden along the income scale presents difficulties. Two main problems arise here: the first concerns the allocation of taxes among the broad groups of decision makers, such as consumers, wage earners, profit earners, etc.; the second concerns the choice of proper criteria for the allocation of taxes among the families along the income scale.

The problem of the allocation of taxes among the broad groups of decision makers is a difficult one to answer because of the unsolved question of shifting, discussed above. Nearly all empirical studies of incidence have employed the traditional assumptions of full shifting to consumers for indirect taxes and of full incidence on factors of production for direct taxes[30]. We shall also concentrate here on the redistributional effects of the VAT substitution under the assumption of complete forward shifting, but allowance will be made for the possibility of partial forward shifting of both the PT and the SET.

Finding proper criteria for the allocation of taxes among the families belonging to different income groups is also a difficult problem. Consumers' expenditure on the various commodities is usually employed for the allocation of indirect taxes. However, when the full forward shifting assumption is dropped, some way of allocating the unshifted part of the tax should be found. This clearly depends upon what happens with the unshifted part of the tax. If it falls on wages, its allocation must be made

[30] Prest has criticized the use of these two assumptions as being inconsistent. See A. R. Prest, 'Statistical Calculations of Tax Burdens', *Economica*, August 1955.

according to the distribution of wages along the income scale. If it falls on profits, the distribution of profits must be used.

Detailed information on the allocation of consumers' expenditure in the UK is provided by the Family Expenditure Survey conducted every year by the Department of Employment. The allocation of consumers' expenditure in the year 1971, as given by the corresponding report for that year, has been used for the allocation of revenues from both the old taxes and the proposed VAT[31]. The unshifted part of the PT and the SET has been allocated on the basis of the allocation of income from each source, information which is also provided in the Family Expenditure Survey.

Fourth, proper measures of income redistribution should be found. Previous works have generally used either of two methods: one consists in a comparison of income distributions before and after the budget change, using some single measure of inequality; the other consists in a comparison of the effective tax, expenditure or budget rates. The first method has the main advantage of providing an answer through a single number which can easily be remembered. It has however the main disadvantage that most people would find it difficult to interpret the Gini coefficients. Besides, Gini coefficients are sometimes misleading[32]. We shall therefore use the effective rates paid by the average family at the various points along the income scale under the old and the new system respectively. These are estimated as follows:

$$t^i = \frac{T^i}{Y^i},$$

where t^i is the effective rate paid by the typical family in the ith income group, T^i is the total tax paid by this family, and Y^i is the family's income under the old tax.

Table 7 presents the amount of tax revenues that the typical household of the various income groups will pay under the assumption of complete forward shifting of all taxes. From the

[31] Allowance has been made for certain known weaknesses of the Family Expenditure Survey Reports as regards consumers' expenditure on drinks and tobacco, where evidence of serious underecording by the families exists. Thus expenditure on drinks has been increased by 50 per cent and expenditure on tobacco has been increased by 25 per cent.

[32] For a discussion of this point see, D. G. M. Dosser, 'Taxation', in *The Economics of Europe*, ed. J. Pinder, Charles Knight, 1972.

results of this table it follows that the substitution of the value-added tax for the PT and the SET will not probably affect the distribution of income substantially especially if drinks and tobacco are brought into VAT. Indeed a comparison of the distributions in columns 1–3 shows that, if a certain amount of revenues was to be raised under either of alternative A–C, the typical household of each income class would pay approximately the same amount, no matter which system is used. On the other hand, if this same amount was to be raised through the VAT, which is not levied on drinks and tobacco (alternative D), the VAT will be slightly more progressive than the PT and the SET. If part of the old taxes was falling backwards on profits the VAT substitution will probably result in a redistribution of income in favour of the lower income groups, since the distribution of profits favours the upper income groups.

Table 7. The incidence of the old and the new tax system in the UK

Income groups weekly income of households in £	Average weekly income	Amount of tax paid by the typical family in £ per week				Effective rates % of average weekly income			
	(1)	A (2)	B (3)	C (4)	D (5)	A (2:1)	B (3:1)	C (4:1)	D (5:1)
under 10	7.89	.30	.30	.32	.33	3.8	3.8	4.1	4.2
10–15	12.40	.52	.52	.53	.53	4.2	4.2	4.3	4.3
15–20	17.55	.73	.74	.80	.78	4.2	4.2	4.6	4.4
20–25	22.52	1.06	1.05	1.03	1.00	4.7	4.7	4.6	4.4
25–30	27.49	1.23	1.25	1.24	1.20	4.5	4.5	4.5	4.5
30–35	32.50	1.50	1.50	1.45	1.40	4.6	4.6	4.5	4.3
35–40	37.45	1.59	1.64	1.59	1.56	4.2	4.4	4.2	4.2
40–45	42.52	1.63	1.65	1.69	1.61	3.8	3.9	4.0	3.8
45–50	47.42	2.09	2.08	2.06	2.06	4.4	4.4	4.3	4.3
50–60	54.69	2.40	2.39	2.36	2.46	4.4	4.4	4.3	4.5
60–80	68.14	2.74	2.72	2.78	2.79	4.0	4.0	4.1	4.1
80 or more	112.26	4.30	4.25	4.24	4.40	3.8	3.8	3.8	3.9

A= tax paid under the 1970 structure of the PT and the SET.
B= tax paid under the 1972 structure of the PT and the SET.
C= tax paid under the VAT with drinks and tobacco brought into the VAT.
D= tax paid under the VAT with drinks and tobacco zero-rated.

Trade effects

Some theoretical aspects of the trade effects of VAT substitution. The substitution of the value-added tax for a pre-existing turnover tax will affect trade in a number of ways. Both exports and imports will probably be affected. The main types of trade effects of VAT substitution are:

(i) Price effects due to over and undercompensation on exports.

Substitution of the value-added tax for a turnover tax will affect trade from the export side, if different export rebates are granted under the two taxes. Thus, provided exports are exactly rebated under the VAT, the effects of tax substitution on exports depend upon whether undercompensation or overcompensation of exports took place under the pre-existing turnover tax. If undercompensation of exports took place under the old turnover tax, the tax substitution will result in a reduction of export prices abroad and consequently an increase in the volume of exports. On the other hand, if exports were overcompensated under the pre-existing turnover tax, the tax substitution will lead to an increase in the price and consequently a reduction in the volume of exports. The change in the volume of exports is given by[33]:

$$dX = e^x \left(\frac{dP}{P}\right) X_0 \qquad (2)$$

where e^x stands for the price elasticity of exports, dP/P stands for the percentage change in the price of exports abroad, and X_0 stands for the pre-tax substitution volume of exports.

The value of exports, however, may either increase or fall, depending not only upon the direction of the change in the volume of exports but also upon the magnitude of the price elasticity of exports. If the price elasticity is greater than unity, the value of exports will change in the same direction with the change in the volume of exports, while if the price elasticity is lower than unity, the value will change in the opposite direction. If the elasticity is unity, the value of exports will remain unaffected.

(ii) Income effects on a country's exports through changes in demand abroad.

Besides the above inter-source substitution or price effects, a country's exports may change because of possible income changes abroad consequent upon the tax substitution in the

[33] This formula is derived from the price elasticity of demand, solved with respect to *dx*.

country under consideration. These effects are given by:

$$dX = m_j^w \, dY^w \qquad (3)$$

where dY^w is the change in world income and m_j^w is the world's marginal propensity to import from the country making the tax substitution. Such effects are not however expected to be very important in the UK case and will not be considered any further.

(iii) Price effects on imports through structural changes in domestic demand. If the value-added tax falls on demand at effective rates different from those at which the pre-existing tax fell, the tax substitution will lead to a change in the structure of demand in the country. This will cause trade effects only if demand is shifted between products with different import contents. Thus if v_i stands for the import content of product i and v_j for the import content of product j, and the tax substitution causes a shift of expenditure from product i to product j amounting to dE, the effect of tax substitution on imports will be given by:

$$dM = v_j dE - v_i dE = (v_j - v_i)\, dE. \qquad (4)$$

If $v_j > v_i$ imports increase; if $v_j = v_i$ imports are not affected by the structural change in demand; and if $v_j < v_i$ imports fall. Estimates of these effects are given in table 8.

(iv) Effects on imports through income changes in the country.

Besides the structure of demand, the tax substitution may also affect the overall level of demand through possible income changes in the country making the tax substitution. This, of course, depends on whether or not the two taxes bring in different amounts of tax revenues. The trade effects due to income changes are given by:

$$dM = m dY, \qquad (5)$$

where m stands for the country's overall marginal propensity to import, and dY denotes the income changes consequent upon the VAT substitution.

(v) Effects on imports through differences in the tax treatment of imports as compared with domestic production under the two taxes.

If the two taxes do not levy the same relative burden on imports and domestic production, the tax substitution will lead to a change in the price of imports relative to the price of domestic production and will cause an inter-source substitution of supply. If the pre-existing turnover tax levies a relative burden on imports higher than that levied by the new tax there will be an increase in imports; if both taxes levy the same relative burden, imports will remain unaffected; while if the new tax discriminates against imports there will follow a reduction in imports. The trade effects of tax substitution from this source are given by:

$$dM = e^m (dP/P) M_0, \quad (6)$$
[34]

where e^m stands for the price elasticity of imports, dP/P stands for the percentage change in the price of imports relative to the price of domestic production and M_0 stands for the pre-tax substitution volume of imports. The estimates of this effect are given in table 9.

(vi) Effects on trade through differential tax treatment of investment.

Finally, the tax substitution will affect the value of imports through changes in the volume of exports. For, the change in exports will necessitate a corresponding change in imports to accommodate the new volume of exports. The change in imports depends upon the change in the volume of exports caused by the tax substitution as well as upon the marginal imports component of exports. Thus, if dX stands for the change in the volume of exports brought about by the tax substitution and m^x stands for the overall marginal imports component of exports, the change in imports resulting from the change in exports will be given by:

$$dM = m^x dX. \quad (7)$$

Trade effects of VAT substitution in the UK: The empirical results. The substitution of the VAT for the PT and the SET in the UK will probably bring about trade effects through all sources discussed above. Thus:

(1) Neither the PT nor the SET are fully rebated on exports. Although the PT is a single stage tax, levied at the wholesale stage and is mostly rebated on exports, a small part of it enters

[34] This formula is derived from the price elasticity of imports, solved with respect to *dM*.

indirectly the cost of domestic production and is not rebated on exports. Similarly the SET is not fully rebated on exports. On the other hand, the VAT is mostly rebated. Only a small part will enter indirectly into the value of exports and remain unrebated. The proposed VAT substitution will therefore result in a reduction in export prices and an increase in the volume and probably the value of exports.

(2) The change in the structure of consumer prices brought about by the tax substitution will cause a change in the structure of consumers' demand in the UK. This will probably affect imports by shifting demand between commodities with different import components as discussed above.

(3) Although the PT treats imports and domestic production alike the SET does not. For the SET falls only on domestic production while imports enter the country untaxed. It is only the tax falling on the distributive trades sector that falls on both domestic production and imports but even this part may discriminate between the two sources of supply if different distribution channels are used in each case. The VAT, on the other hand, treats domestic production and imports truly alike. The proposed VAT substitution in the UK will therefore result in a reduction in the price of domestic production relative to the price of imports. This will make imports more expensive and will result in substitution of domestic production for imports which will tend to improve the balance of trade.

(4) The proposed VAT substitution will also affect trade through overall income changes in the UK, consequent upon the tax substitution. The size of the income changes and therefore the magnitude of the trade changes thereon depend upon the tax rate that will be finally adopted in the UK as well as upon what the government is going to do with the extra revenues that it will receive, if the VAT is levied at a rate higher than the one that would bring in equal yield. Will the government spend it, save it or effect compensatory reductions in other taxes? The answer to this question clearly depends upon many factors other than the pure decision to change from the PT and the SET over to the VAT. Demand management considerations, a desire to change the mix of direct and indirect taxes, or that of general and special consumption taxes, may be

some of the possible factors that will determine the size of the actual rate that will finally be adopted. For this reason, we shall leave income effects as well as the trade effects thereon out of this exercise, concentrating on the trade effects resulting from the pure structural change in taxes.

(5) Finally, a substantial part of both the PT and of the SET fall on investment. This inflates the cost of capital and, provided market conditions allow it, results in price increases through capital depreciation. This part discriminates against domestic production as compared with imports and against the country's exports abroad. The VAT, on the other hand, falls on consumption while investment expenditure is effectively exempted. Consequently the abolition of the PT and the SET in the longer-run, when full equilibrium under the VAT will have been achieved, will result in a further increase in the price of imports relative to the price of domestic production in the UK and a reduction in the price of the UK exports abroad. This will lead to inter-source substitution effects from both the import and the export sides, reducing the value of imports and probably increasing the value of exports, thereby tending to improve the balance of trade from both sides.

For the estimation of some of the above trade effects we need: (i) relative price changes of the various groups of consumer goods and services caused by the VAT substitution in the UK; (ii) price elasticities of consumers' expenditure in the UK; (iii) the import components of the various groups of consumer goods and services; (iv) price elasticities of demand for imports and of exports; and (v) the increase in the price of the UK imports relative to the price of domestic production and the reduction in the price of exports caused by the tax substitution. To this we now turn.

(i) Relative price changes of consumer goods and services in the UK. The relative changes in the prices of the various categories of consumer goods and services in the UK have already been estimated and set out on table 6.

(ii) Price elasticities of consumer goods and services in the UK. Price elasticities for a large number of groups of consumer goods and services in the UK are presented in column 1 of table 8 below. The estimates were obtained from regressions, using the Stone and Row dynamic model of quantities consumed on total consumption and relative prices[35].

Table 8. Price elasticities, import components and import changes resulting from the structural change in consumers' expenditure in the UK

Group of Consumers' Expenditure	Price elasticities of consumer demand in the UK	Import component in 1968	Imports changes	
			Base year rates 1970	Base year rates 1972
1. Food	−0.54	31.2	24.6	31.0
2. Drink	−0.48	6.9	−6.8	−5.6
3. Tobacco	−0.45	8.1	−5.9	−4.7
4. Housing	−0.61	4.0	−0.4	−0.7
5. Fuel and light	−1.03	11.0	—	—
6. Clothing and footwear	−0.29	19.1	0.4	−0.4
7. Motor cars and motor cycles	−1.27	12.6	8.2	−2.8
8. Furniture and floor coverings	−1.56	16.6	7.5	4.9
9. Radio, electrical, etc.	−1.20	16.1	17.0	8.3
10. Other household goods	−1.13	21.0	−3.9	−5.0
11. Books, newspapers, etc.	−0.44	15.0	—	—
12. Chemists' goods	−0.53	15.4	6.1	3.1
13. Miscellaneous recreational goods	−2.08	17.0	10.2	—
14. Other miscellaneous goods	−0.80	20.3	13.0	7.5
15. Running costs of motor vehicles	−1.24	9.4	−1.8	—
16. Travel	−0.97	11.6	—	—
17. Communication services	−0.64	6.0	−0.7	—
18. Entertainment	−0.55	26.1	−0.2	−2.0
19. Other services	−0.89	5.7	−5.8	−4.7
20. Consumers' expenditure abroad	−2.73	100.0	6.8	29.9
Total	—	16.5	68.3	58.8

(iii) The import components of consumer goods and services in the UK. The import components incorporated into the various categories of consumers' expenditure in the UK have been estimated on the basis of information provided by the input-output tables for the UK[36]. Both the direct and the indirect components have been taken into account. The former refers

[35] For a description of the model see R. D. Stone and D. A. Row, 'The Durability of Consumer Durable Goods', *Econometrica*, 1960. For a discussion of the data used and the detailed results obtained see T. Georgakopoulos. *Indirect Tax Harmonization in Economic Unions with Special Reference to the EEC and the UK* (Ph.D. dissertation submitted to the University of York, February 1971, unpublished).

[36] See Central Statistical Office, *Input-Output Tables for the UK*, 1968.

to the value of the final products imported ready for final use, while the latter refers to the value of imports used indirectly as primary inputs in the production of consumer goods in the UK. The results obtained are presented in column 2 of table 8.

(iv) Price elasticities of demand for imports in the UK and of the UK's exports abroad. Econometric analyses of the demand for imports in the UK have not produced satisfactory estimates of the price coefficient. A number of recent studies have failed to find a significant price effect[37]. Recent studies concerning the import surcharge seems to support the hypothesis that the UK imports are not very sensitive to price changes. Johnston and Henderson, for example, have estimated the probable import savings from the introduction of the import surcharge during the period October 1964 to December 1965 to amount to something between 1 and 2 per cent of the total import bill[38]. This estimate implies a tariff elasticity of imports in the UK lying between −0.1 and −0.2. In view of this lack of evidence concerning the price elasticity of the UK imports, three alternative estimates of price elasticities will be employed here. A low elasticity of −0.5, an intermediate elasticity of −1.2, and a higher elasticity of −1.8.

Contrary to the analysis of the UK imports, recent econometric investigation of the UK's exports seems to indicate the presence of an effective price mechanism. Ball et al., for example, found a significant price effect on the UK's exports, when the share of the country's exports to the total trade in manufactures was used as the dependent variable[39]. The elasticity estimates obtained range between −1.40 and −2.0, when alternative measures for the pressure of domestic demand were used in the equation. Houthakker and Magee[40], on the other hand,

---

[37] See for example H. S. Houthakker and S. R. Magee, 'Income and Price Elasticities in International Trade', *The Review of Economics and Statistics*, May 1969. For a good discussion of the problems encountered in estimating price elasticities of imports and a survey of the literature, see S. J. Prais, *Econometric Research in International Trade: A Review*, Kyklos, 1962.

[38] See J. Johnston and M. Henderson, 'Assessing the Effects of the Import Surcharge', *Manchester School*, May 1967.

[39] See R. J. Ball, J. R. Eaton and M. D. Stener, 'The Relationship between United Kingdom Export Performance in Manufacturing and the International Pressure of Demand', *Economic Journal*, Vol. 76, 1966.

[40] Op. cit.

have not found a significant price effect on total exports. To give the possible variation of the trade effects from the export side, we shall also employ the three alternative values of price elasticities employed with respect to imports.

(v) The changes in the price of imports and exports in the UK. The increase in the price of imports relative to the price of domestic production in the UK as well as the reduction in the price of the UK exports abroad will again depend upon the degree of forward shifting at the PT and the SET[41]. If the PT and the SET are fully shifted forward, the price of imports relative to the price of domestic production will increase by about 1.2 per cent of the pre-substitution price of imports, while the price of exports will fall by about −0.8 per cent[42]. If the PT and the SET are only partially shifted on to prices, the VAT substitution will lead to a lower increase in the relative price of imports, and a lower reduction in the relative price of exports. Finally, if the PT and the SET are not shifted forward at all, the VAT substitution will leave the relative price of both imports and exports unchanged.

We now come to the estimates of some of the trade effects in the UK. The trade effects resulting from the VAT substitution in the UK are presented in columns 3–4 of table 8 and in table 9. From the results in table 8, we see that the structural change in consumers' expenditure following the tax substitution leads to an increase in the value of imports, but this effect cannot be considered to be substantial in detrimentally affecting the UK balance of payments. Indeed, the change in imports that will follow the structural change in consumers' expenditure as result of the VAT substitution is estimated to amount to £68.3 million when the 1970 structure of the PT and the SET is used as the basis and £58.8 million, when the 1972 structure of the PT and the SET is used as the basis.

---

[41] The VAT is, as before, assumed to be completely shifted on to product prices.

[42] The comparison is here made with the situation under the 1970 rates of the PT and the SET. If the 1972 tax rates are considered, the price changes will be smaller. Thus, the increase in the price of imports is in this case estimated to amount to 0.65 per cent and the reduction in the price of exports to −0.5. The model through which these price changes have been derived is presented in T. Georgakopoulos, 'Trade Effects of Tax Substitution', op. cit.

The trade effects resulting from inter-sources substitution will, on the other hand, lead to an improvement in the balance of payments, especially if the elasticity of exports and imports are quite high. As shown in table 9, the net value of exports (after allowance is made for the required amount of imports to produce the higher volume of exports) will increase only if the elasticity is high. Imports will fall whatever the elasticity value, however, but the reduction will be greater the larger the elasticity. The trade effects from the inter-source substitution of supply will be smaller if a comparison with the situation under the 1972 tax rates is made because, as shown above, the relative price changes of imports and exports will be lower.

Table 9. Trade effects resulting from the inter-source substitution of supply (in £mn)

	Value of UK trade in 1970	Trade changes compared with the situation under the 1970 rates			Trade changes compared with the situation under the 1972 rates		
		l.e.	i.e.	h.e.	l.e.	i.e.	h.e.
Export Side	11,182	−52.5	−1.7	41.7	−32.8	−1.1	26.1
Import Side	10,898	−66.5	−159.6	−239.3	−35.4	−84.9	−127.3
Balance of trade (exports-imports)	284	14.0	157.9	281.0	2.6	83.8	153.4

Note: l.e.=low elasticity −0.5; i.e.=intermediate elasticity −1.2; and h.e.=high elasticity −1.8.

From what calculations can be made, the introduction of VAT has a favourable influence on the UK balance of trade. With high values of price elasticities assumed, and a comparison made with 1970 rates of PT, the total effect through price changes in groups of products amounts to an improvement of £213 (£281–68) million. This constitutes about 2 per cent of the value of UK trade. The effect is, of course, reduced if the price elasticities of total imports and exports are lower, or if the PT and SET are shifted forward to a lesser extent.

This is only a partial view of the effects on the UK balance of trade of the introduction of VAT. The effects through more complete rebating of tax paid on exported goods, noted as (1) at the beginning of this section, and the effect through the treatment of investment, described under (5), both lend weight to the proposition that the substitution of VAT for PT and SET will have a favourable influence on the trade account of the British balance of payments.

Conclusions

Though the results depend on (a) the rates, (b) the shifting, and (c) the administration in practice, of old and new taxes in the tax change under study, the effects on prices, income distribution, and trade can never be said to be large overall. This is true of the effect on the retail price index, the change in the after-tax distribution, and in the trade balance.

This is perhaps not surprising when it is remembered that the tax change is an equal-yield one (confirmed by the choice of the 10 per cent basic rate in the 1973 budget). Overall effects are likely to be great if the tax substitution involves a significant change in yield, or a radical change in the form of taxation, for example, between indirect and direct taxation.

Whilst the broad, or macroeconomic, changes are not great, of course, on a microeconomic scale, our type of analysis cannot reveal the effects on certain product prices, on certain income groups, which may well be serious for those concerned.

Our analysis is an ex ante one at a moment when the VAT is just on the point of introduction. It will take, perhaps, some two years to see the administration of the VAT settle down, and some of its effects become apparent. An export appraisal of our results will, unfortunately, be complicated by the rapid rate of change in prices and money incomes occurring through other causes at the same time.

Probably the introduction of VAT will get the blame for many of these undesired inflationary movements. Our ex ante analysis may help as a rebuttal that so many crimes can be ascribed to this offender.

3
Excise Duties

John Dodsworth

Introduction

In this chapter we shall be considering prospective EEC plans for the harmonization of excise duties and relating these to the present structure of duties in the UK. In doing so we shall depart to some extent from the approach and format of the previous chapter on value-added taxation. This is partly the result of having to deal with a number of separate taxes, each with their own distinct problems, rather than with one general tax. Mainly, however, the difference in approach reflects the fact that the harmonization of excise duties is at a much earlier stage of development than that of the VAT. Whilst quite substantial progress has been made toward the introduction of a community-wide value-added tax, it was not until February 1972 that the first comprehensive Proposal on the harmonization of excise duties appeared.

As a consequence of this, no large-scale changes in excise duties will be immediately necessary as a result of UK membership. Only some minor modifications will be required, and these stem from the introduction of the VAT; from the introduction of the Common External Tariff; and from the elimination of various types of discrimination which currently operate against imports of excisable products. Positive measures to harmonize the structure of excise duties have still to be approved by the Member States.

Arguments in favour of harmonization emphasize the 'protective' aspect of excise duties. Thus the European Commission in its Proposal claims that structural and rate differences conspire to distort competition and limit the free movement of goods between Member States. But this is only one, and generally a subsidiary, aspect of excise duties. They are first and foremost revenue raisers and this, of course, tends to act against any movement to harmonization. In each of the EEC countries receipts from excise duties form a significant proportion of total revenue, and this is particularly the case in the UK. In the UK, duties on tobacco, petroleum and alcoholic drinks account for almost a quarter of central government revenue. In assessing a harmonization proposal, therefore, particularly with a view to alignment of tax rates, the most important consideration is likely to be the effect on revenue. Any proposal which necessitates other than a marginal fall in revenue seems certain to meet with resistance from the country involved.

A further consideration, which reinforces the argument above, and would normally act against harmonization, concerns the nature of the products taxed. The excise duties with which we shall be mainly concerned are sumptuary taxes. They are based on, or at least imply, certain social values. Thus, as an obvious example, duty is levied on tobacco not solely for its revenue potential but also on the presumption that increased consumption would be detrimental to the health of the community. On these grounds, unless we can forsee an EEC viewpoint on these matters, there may also be resistance to any substantial changes in rates of excise duty.

Bearing in mind the factors outlined above, this chapter has been divided into four parts. In the first part we shall be examining the initial changes required in the UK system of excise duties as a result of membership of the EEC. These changes, as mentioned above, are connected with the introduction of VAT and the conversion of excise duties into internal taxes. In the second part we shall consider briefly the background to, and the substance of, the EEC's 1972 Proposal for the harmonization of excise duties. This is followed in part three with a product-by-product comparison of rates and structure of excise duties in the UK and the EEC countries, and an assessment of the relevance of the 1972, and earlier, Commission Proposals. Finally, in part four, we shall consider some possible price, revenue and distributional aspects of movements toward harmonization.

I. INITIAL CHANGES REQUIRED IN THE UK SYSTEM OF EXCISE DUTIES

The Introduction of VAT

Value-added tax will be introduced in the UK in April 1973. As a result of this it seems likely that some changes will be made in current rates of excise duty although, as made clear in the previous chapter, precise details of this have not yet been announced.

VAT is scheduled to be levied on some excisable products, i.e. tobacco, beer, wine, and spirits, but not on petroleum. All fuel and power, including hydrocarbon oils, will at least initially be zero-rated. The question which the government is leaving open at the moment is whether value-added tax will be levied on top of the present excise duty or whether it will be substituted for the top segment of the present excise duty. The latter course, involving a reduction in the rate of duty whilst maintaining the same overall burden of taxation, seems likely if only because of the government's preoccupation with inflation. But this course does have other advantages in the longer-term context of harmonization. It will become clear in this paper that in general excise duties in the UK are levied at a higher rate than corresponding duties in other Member States. Any reduction in the current UK level will, therefore, make easier an eventual alignment of rates throughout the Community if this is to be a desired outcome.

Conversion to an Internal Tax

Whatever the fate of the latest Proposal for harmonization, the structure of UK excise duties will have to undergo some modification during the transitional period of membership. This is to keep them in accord with the provisions of the Treaty of Rome. The guiding principle of the fiscal provisions of the Treaty is stated in Article 95, i.e. 'A member state shall not impose directly or indirectly on the products of other member states any internal charges of any kind in excess of those applied directly or indirectly to similar domestic products.' This sort of discrimination between imports and domestic products can emerge both from different rates being charged and from imposing different bases of assessment. In a mild form both sorts of discrimination are present under the existing system of UK excise duties. This was recognized in the July 1971 White Paper which dealt with conditions of UK entry[1]. Paragraph 133 states that 'during the course of the transitional period our present customs duties (on hydrocarbon oils, beer, spirits, wines and tobacco) will need to be converted into internal taxes in order to conform with the Treaty of Rome'. For imports of these products from outside the Community the Common External Tariff will be applicable and this may be substituted for part of the present tax.

At present various preference systems operate on excisable products, favouring not only domestic but also EFTA, AIFTA and Commonwealth goods. A listing of revenue obtained under the different rates is provided in table 1. For the most part the preferential margins that exist are small and the revenue consequences of introducing parity of treatment will be relatively minor.

Taking tobacco first, duty in the UK is based on imports of leaf tobacco assessed according to weight and moisture content. The basic rate for tobacco leaf containing not less than 10 per cent moisture is £5.041 per lb. But, imports from the Commonwealth, EFTA and AIFTA are entitled to a preference margin of 7.7p per lb.[2]. This applies to well over half of UK imports of unmanufactured tobacco. If all imports were to be taxed at the full rate then revenue would be increased by approximately £8.5 million. However, this represents, as can be seen from table 1, something less than 1 per cent of total tobacco revenue.

For beer, wines and spirits different rates of tax are again applied to domestic produce, imports from EFTA and the Commonwealth, and imports from other sources. The unit of charge on beer is the bulk barrel (36 gallons) whilst the amount of duty is calculated according to the strength or specific gravity[3]. On imports of beer not of Commonwealth or EFTA origin there is a surcharge of £1.00 per barrel. Commonwealth

[1] *The United Kingdom and the European Communities*, Cmnd 4715, HMSO, 1971.
[2] A similar system of preferences is applied to various kinds of imported manufactured tobacco.
[3] This is outlined in greater detail in part three of the paper.

and EFTA imports, which account for over 90 per cent of the total, are charged the same rate as domestically produced beer. The remaining imports consist mainly of lager and hence the surcharge may currently give some measure of protection to the British lager industry[4].

Table 1. Receipts from UK excise duties 1970/71: Categorized by source (in £mn)

	Domestic	Preferential	EFTA/AIFTA	Full rate	Total
Tobacco	—	571.34	2.72	568.30	1,142.4
Spirits	283.80	40.20	0.41	47.30	371.7
Wines	17.90	11.09	—	63.96	92.9
Beer	442.00	18.04	5.36	1.68	467.1
Hydrocarbon Oil	—	—	—	1,395.80	1,395.8

Source: 62nd Report of the Commissioners of Her Majesty's Custom and Excise for the year ended 31 March 1971, Cmnd 4826.

Duty on spirits reflects a similar situation. Commonwealth and EFTA imports are charged with the same basic rate as the domestically produced good (£18.85 per proof gallon) whilst spirits imported from other countries are liable to an additional duty of 12.5p per proof gallon. Roughly this means that a preferential rate is charged on imports which comprise mainly of rum, whilst other imports, mainly brandy and liqueurs, attract the full rate of duty.

Finally, in the case of wine the picture is somewhat more complicated. Not only are there separate rates for imports from different areas but also for heavy wines and light wines, and for still wines and sparkling wines. Furthermore, the dividing line between light and heavy wine, which depends on the proof spirit content, differs according to whether the wine comes from within the UK or from the Commonwealth (in which case it is 27 degrees proof), or whether it is from any other source (in which case it is 25 degrees proof). The duty rates on still wine, which accounts for most of the revenue, are £1.61 per gallon (light wine) and £2.71 per gallon (heavy wine). For light wines preference margins are quite small, being 12.5p per gallon for British wine and 10p a gallon for Commonwealth

[4] 62nd Report of the Commissioners of HM Customs and Excise, Cmnd 4826, p. 60, HMSO, 1972.

wine. However, for heavy wines the margins are more substantial. Duty is levied on British wine at 97.5p a gallon below the standard rate and on Commonwealth wine at 50p per gallon below the standard rate.

It is interesting to note that the EEC have accepted some instances where tax arrangements favour domestically produced goods. In Germany, for example, there is a refund of excise duty on bottles of sparkling wine providing that at least 75 per cent of the basic wine used is of German origin. The Commission decided in this case that the refund was not a matter for Article 95 of the Treaty of Rome and that it should be regarded as aid to the German wine growing industry. It therefore comes under Article 93 of the Treaty.

II. BACKGROUND TO THE COMMISSION'S 1972 PROPOSAL ON THE HARMONIZATION OF EXCISE DUTIES

Previous Proposals

Although the 1972 Proposal was undoubtedly more comprehensive than those Proposals which preceded it, it did incorporate earlier proposals and can be seen as the culmination of preparatory work spanning over a decade.

As long ago as June 1959 a Working Group (No. 3) was set up to enquire into the problems involved in excise duty harmonization. At the outset it became clear that not only were there many technical and revenue difficulties to be resolved but also that there would be significant overlaps with other Community and national policies. It was felt, for instance, that the question of excise duties on manufactured tobacco could best be tackled alongside the associated problems of trade in raw tobacco and the internal distribution of tobacco products. The framework Proposal regarding measures to be taken in the tobacco sector was finally sent from the European Commission to the Council in 1967. It dealt with four related areas:

(a) the establishment of a common market in unmanufactured tobacco in accordance with the Common Agricultural Policy;
(b) the harmonization of taxes other than VAT levied on the consumption of manufactured tobacco;

(c) the abolition of commercial monopolies in tobacco which exist in Italy and France;
(d) the treatment of imports of tobacco from the Yaounde states and associated overseas countries.

On the harmonization issue raised by this Proposal little progress was made, and it was widely predicted that no compromise agreement would be possible among the Member States. On 20 November 1970, however, a revised draft was submitted by the Commission and on this Proposal agreement was reached *in principle*. On the basis of this latter Proposal the 1972 Proposal calls for the harmonization of excise duties on manufactured tobaccos by 1 January 1974.

The other tangible evidence of progress prior to the 1972 Proposal relates to excise duties levied on mineral oils. The Commission has approached this tax from two different standpoints. Firstly, as regards duty on petroleum used as motor fuel, there is a plan in existence (proposed by the Commission, 29 March 1971) for receipts from a harmonized tax to be incorporated into a general rate which is to be utilized in the joint financing of infrastructures. The harmonization of this tax, therefore, appears to be closely tied to the development of the Common Transport Policy. Secondly, as regards taxes on those mineral oils which are used as fuels (in boilers, furnaces, etc.) a separate draft resolution was prepared and presented to the Council on 28 December 1970. This Proposal specified an alignment of nominal tax rates throughout the Community and was intended primarily as one element in the formation of a Common Energy Policy. Again, as with tobacco, the 1972 Proposal uses these proposals as a basis for its recommendation that all mineral oils should be subject to harmonized excise duties by 1 January 1974.

Coverage of Excise Duties

The first question to be considered by the 1972 Proposal relates to which of existing excise duties should be retained and harmonized and which should be abolished. It is to this aspect that we turn first.

Those duties which are levied on mineral oils, tobacco, beer, wines and spirits we shall refer to as 'traditional' excises. With one or two exceptions these are taxes imposed throughout the

EEC in one form or another[5]. Together, as can be seen from table 2, they account for the bulk of revenue collected from consumption taxes other than VAT.

There are, however, a number of taxes to be considered besides the traditional excise duties. In the Benelux countries, for instance, there is an excise duty on sugar; in France there are special taxes imposed on the consumption of tea, cocoa and spices. In both Germany and Italy a wide variety of products are subject to excise duties[6].

Such taxes as these present a problem to those responsible for drafting harmonization proposals. The simplest expedient would seem to be their abolition, and this is the solution favoured in the Commission's report. However, the abolition of these taxes could pose certain revenue, difficulties for Germany and perhaps for Italy[7]. On the other hand there are a number of arguments against the introduction of new taxes into the remaining member countries. As the Commission's Proposal points out, the introduction of duties on coffee and tea would be inadvisable, as both are primarily products from developing countries and such action would certainly be contrary to the aims of UNCTAD. Similarly the Commission argues that it is no longer desirable to maintain excise duties on sugar as they affect a good which is 'partly an essential product and partly a raw material for industry'. More details from the Commission's viewpoint on the coverage of excise duties are included in chapter 6.

The February 1972 Proposal suggests that even as regards neutrality of competition it is unnecessary to insist on exactly the same coverage in each Member State. National excise duties may remain in existence providing only that border tax adjustments and frontier controls are removed. Thus, there are about twenty different consumption taxes—in addition to the traditional excise duties—which could theoretically be main-

[5] The exceptions are wine in Italy and non-sparkling wine in Germany. A consumption tax on beer was introduced in France in 1969.

[6] In Germany there are duties on sugar, coffee, tea, salt, lighting equipment, matches, playing cards and acetic acid. In Italy there are duties on sugar, sweeteners, coffee, cocoa, margarine, matches, bananas, methane gas, animal and vegetable oils.

[7] In Italy separate taxes may be incorporated into VAT when this is introduced.

Table 2. Receipts from consumption taxes other than VAT and general sales taxes in the UK and EEC, 1969 (million u.a.)[a]

	Belgium	France	Germany	Nether.	Italy	UK[b]
Mineral oils	415.2	2,249.3	2,896.5	442.8	2,471.5	3,142.8
Tobacco[c]	162.2	752.7	1,710.1	235.6	1,156.7	2,764.8
Alcohol	48.7	386.2	585.3	114.4	100.1	797.0
Wines	15.9	84.3	58.5	13.3	—	193.4
Beer[d]	49.0	26.1	322.1	37.3	44.1	1,081.2
Traditional Excises as % of total	99.4	99.9	93.4	97.7	89.2	100.0
Sugar	4.0	—	33.6	19.6	75.6	—
Coffee	—	0.2	309.3	—	120.9	—
Tea	—	0.1	10.4	—	—	—
Cocoa	—	1.0	—	—	10.6	—
Salt	—	—	11.2	—	35.0	—
Miscellaneous	—	0.4	26.5	—	212.8	—

Source: EEC Proposals for Harmonizing Consumer Taxes other than VAT *Bulletin of the European Communities Supplement* 3/72. 62nd Report of the Commissioners of Her Majesty's Custom and Excise for year ended 31 March 1971, Cmnd 4826.

Notes: [a] For ease of comparison throughout this paper national currencies will be converted into units of account (u.a.) according to the following rates: £0.41667, 625 lire, DM 3.66, 5.5549 Ffr, 50 Bfr, 3.62 Guld.

[b] UK figures are for financial year 1969/70.

[c] Including cigarette papers and smoking requisites where applicable.

[d] Including mineral waters where applicable.

tained, providing that there are no tax rebates for those products when exported to other Member States and that no excise duty is payable on them when imported from other Member States. This would seem to be a workable solution only if the rates of duty are sufficiently low. As pointed out elsewhere, different shopping patterns may emerge in frontier areas and possibly beyond—for example, a West German could buy coffee in the Netherlands and no longer have to pay duty at the West German border[8].

The 1972 Proposed Directive

The 1972 Proposed Directive states in Article 3 that by 1 January 1974 at the latest the Member States shall subject the tradi-

[8] *European Trends*, May 1972.

tional excisable products to harmonized duties. The methods of harmonizing existing taxes will be the subject of future directives to be adopted by the Council. A broad description of the Proposal can be found in chapter 6.

As for the details of the harmonization of traditional excise duties, new Proposals have been drawn up for taxes on alcohol, wine and beer, which, along with the previous Proposals on tobacco and mineral oils outlined above, will be more closely examined in the following sections. It should perhaps be stressed that at the time of writing no Council decision has been recorded on the harmonization Proposals and that, therefore, there is considerable doubt whether the Commission's timetable will be fulfilled. Certainly the Proposals do raise a number of contentious issues and, as we shall see, their acceptance would involve major changes in the structure of UK excise duties.

The present Proposals mainly concern tax structures rather than rates, but in what follows we shall be anticipating the difficulties arising from an alignment of tax rates by considering also the divergence of rates of excise duty as between Member States.

III. A COMPARISON OF EXCISE DUTIES IN THE UK AND THE EEC: THE RELEVANCE OF THE COMMISSION'S PROPOSALS

Mineral Oils

In terms of revenue the most important excise duty in each of the countries considered is that on mineral oils. In the UK, Belgium, France and W. Germany, taxes on mineral oils provide between 8 and 10 per cent of central government revenue[9]. In the Netherlands receipts are relatively less important, whereas in Italy approximately 18 per cent of government revenue comes from this source[10].

As stated in Section I the European Commission has approached mineral oil taxes from two different standpoints—one from the point of view of a Common Transport Policy, the

---

[9] The introduction of VAT into the UK will not alter this as the fuel and power sector is initially to be zero-rated.

[10] In addition, in Italy a small percentage of receipts accrue directly to local government.

other from the point of view of a Common Energy Policy. Two Proposals have been sent to the Council. The first, which was forwarded on 28 December 1970, provided for the harmonization of those taxes levied on hydrocarbon oils which were to be used as combustibles. This was followed in March 1971 by a proposed decision regarding duties levied on motor fuels.

The latter proposal was part of a plan designed to institute a Common Transport Policy. Briefly stated, the Commission believes that at present national transport economies are 'compartmentalized' to an extent which affects distribution of traffic flows and ultimately the location of production. One aspect of this relates to the development of infrastructures, another to the conditions of competition within transport markets.

The Commission's Proposal had three main objectives:

(a) To ensure the optimal utilization of infrastructures from a social viewpoint;
(b) To obtain sufficient revenue to finance the construction, maintenance and management of infrastructures; and
(c) To apportion infrastructure costs in a balanced manner between the different methods of transport and user categories.

To attain these objectives in the case of road transport a direct road tax would be introduced (with pricing at marginal social cost) which would be payable at the time and place where road space was used. To supplement this, in order to cover total cost, revenue would be obtained from harmonized systems of taxes on road vehicles and taxes on motor fuels. The structure and level of these taxes would then be determined according to the requirements of the pricing system, i.e. on the basis of maintaining a balanced budget.

This is clearly an ambitious plan which, even if accepted in principle, could not be operational for many years to come. A preliminary step, however, would be the harmonization of duties on motor fuels and this is in accord with the Commission's views on harmonizing conditions of competition in the transport market. To consider the immediate difficulties involved in the harmonization of duties on petroleum the present rates of tax in the EEC and the UK are shown in table 3.

Table 3. Taxes on Motor Spirit in the UK and EEC 1970/71

(u.a. per gallon)

	Sales price	Total tax	Specific tax	VAT rate[a]	Total tax sales price
Italy	1.02	0.90	0.85	4.2%	88.2%
France	0.96	0.69	0.51	23.0%	71.9%
Belgium	0.88	0.63	0.49	18.0%	71.6%
Netherlands	0.81	0.54	0.52[b]	4.0%	66.7%
United Kingdom	0.80	0.54	0.54	—	67.5%
W. Germany	0.79	0.52	0.48	11.0%	66.2%

Source: For EEC, 'Energy Statistics', 1971 Yearbook.
For UK, 62nd Report Customs and Excise 1971, ibid.

Notes: [a] For Italy this shows the IGE rate of tax.
[b] Reduced to 0.51 u.a. per gallon from 1 July 1972.

In comparison with taxes in the other EEC countries the UK tax on petroleum is low. Only in Germany is the total tax element less than 0.54 u.a. per gallon. It would seem, therefore, that an alignment of EEC tax rates would entail, if anything, a rise in the UK excise duty on petrol. But this straightforward comparison is complicated by the presence of VAT in some countries and by tax in Italy. As can be seen from the table the ad valorem rates applied in these countries vary considerably—from 4 per cent in the Netherlands to 23 per cent in France. Much of the variation in the total tax element is accounted for by these differences.

In the UK only a specific duty is imposed and in consequence this is higher than similar taxes imposed in many of the other countries. However, with the exception of Italy, these specific duties are already fairly closely aligned. Whether they are to be raised or lowered depends to a large extent on the policy adopted as regards the harmonization of VAT rates. When value-added tax was introduced into the UK in April 1973 petroleum products were zero-rated[11]. Later on, however, it seems likely that a harmonized 'mixed' excise system will be adopted—partly ad valorem and partly specific—and that this will imply an increase in the UK total tax rate on petrol.

As regards the structure of mineral oil taxes there are considerable differences in complexity. At present the system

[11] *Value-Added Tax: Scope and Coverage,* HM Customs and Excise, Notice 701.

adopted in the UK is comparatively simple. There is one basic rate (assessed in terms of gallons) which is levied on all imported oil. Subsequently a rebate system operates for certain types of oil, and for oil put to certain specified uses duty is repaid in full. For rebated oils the basic rate of 0.54 u.a. per gallon is reduced to 0.024 u.a. per gallon. This reduced rate applies to heavy oils such as fuel oil, gas oil and kerosene, but does not apply to oils intended for use as fuel in road vehicles, which bear the full amount of the duty.

One of the principles laid down in the Commission's 1972 Proposal was that excise duties should avoid affecting products which are used as raw materials in industry. As mineral oils may enter into manufacturing costs in a number of ways, exemptions from duty are an important consideration in harmonization plans. In the UK, exemptions have been granted for some time on oil used in fishing boats, lifeboats and ships in home waters, as well as for certain horticultural purposes. Since September 1964 relief from duty has been applied to oil used as a raw material, a solvent, extractant, preservative, or finish in the manufacture of any article. Finally, in September 1969, this list of uses was further extended, although exemption is still not granted for oil used either as a fuel or, with certain exceptions, as a lubricant.

In the EEC countries there are correspondingly more complicated schemes of taxation involving for the most part a larger number of tax rates. These rates are applied according to type of oil and category of use. A full description of the taxes involved would be beyond the scope of this paper.

For most countries, including the UK, exemption from tax is granted for those mineral oils exported or used in industry otherwise than as a motor fuel, lubricating oil or as a combustible. In France, however, all heavy fuel oil is completely free of duty. Special treatment is often afforded to oil used for heating and lighting by private persons. In the Netherlands no duty is paid on this item, whilst in Italy there is a reduced rate applied to oil intended for domestic heating.

Special provision is also made in some countries for agricultural and horticultural uses. In Belgium and Luxembourg there is a reduced rate for gas oil used in engines fitted on agricultural machinery. In Italy complete exemption is granted for oil used in generating electricity for agricultural establishments and for oil used in the direct driving of agricultural machinery such as tractors, combine harvesters, etc. Finally, in the Netherlands relief from duty is extended to those mineral oils used in the preparation of horticultural produce for export and to those used in heating so as to promote the growth of such produce.

These concessions as well as a myriad of lesser regulations need to be taken into account in any harmonization plan.

The Commission's 1970 Proposal, regarding hydrocarbon oils to be used as fuel, was concerned primarily with rates of tax, and in this respect differed from other proposals which have concentrated on structure and left till a later date the specification of rates. Basically the 1970 Proposal stipulated that by 1 January 1976 taxes on fuel oils should be reduced to not more than:

(i) 2 u.a. per metric ton for heavy fuel oils; and
(ii) 5 u.a. per metric ton for light fuel oils.

The proposal was part of a plan to institute an integrated energy policy for the Community. As with many of its policies the Commission has been quick to stress the necessity of first attaining a common internal market. It claims that the alignment of specific taxes on liquid fuels is based mainly on the need to avoid distortions of competition between the various sources of energy within the Community.

To assess the importance of the Commission's proposal the specific tax rates applied at present to fuel oils are set out in table 4. As can be seen from this table, tax rates in several of

Table 4. Specific taxes on fuel oils in the UK and EEC: 1970
(u.a. per metric ton)

	Belgium	France	Germany	Nether.	Italy	UK[b]
Heavy fuels	2.0	—	6.8	3.8	4.0	7.0
Medium fuels	10.8	4.0	2.7	[a]	8.0	—
Light fuels	8.4	4.0	2.7	—	5.9	5.7

Source: European Taxation II/22, February 1971.

Notes: [a] Medium fuels used for heating by private persons are exempted from taxation; those used by businesses are taxed at a rate of 14.6 u.a. per metric ton.

[b] As the UK tax is levied on a different basis of assessment—volume rather than weight—the figures shown are necessarily approximate and are included only as a guide.

the member countries diverge considerably from the proposed rates. What is immediately obvious is that the plan implies a fall in tax rates in each of the countries with the exception of France. In France the present rates already conform with the Commission's Proposal, as the duty on heavy fuel oil has been abolished. In the UK, as in the other EEC countries, the Commission's plan would seem likely to result in a loss of revenue. This was the main complaint raised in a report by M. de Broglie prepared for the European Parliament. According to this report revenue losses in Belgium, Germany, Italy and the Netherlands would exceed 400 million u.a. in 1976 if the Commission's plan was put into operation on schedule. The countries most affected would be Germany (181 million u.a.) and Italy (145 million u.a.). Revenue from rebated heavy oil in the UK accounts for something less than one tenth of total net receipts from hydrocarbon oils (about £132 million). This could be seriously reduced, by up to one half, if the Commission's proposals were accepted.

In answer to the complaints of revenue loss the Commission has claimed that the decrease in revenue would be compensated for by increased consumption. This is true only to the extent that revenue loss will be moderated by increased demand. The difficulty involved in forecasting energy requirements gives rise, however, to an associated problem. If there are high substitution elasticities between different sources of fuel then there are obvious dangers in tackling isolated sections of the market. A movement towards a common internal market for liquid fuels must be assessed in terms of its effects on the competitive position of other fuels. The de Broglie report calls for a more integrated approach and suggests that taxes should be harmonized on all energy sources as a function of their heating power[12].

Tobacco

Following the Commission's 1967 Proposal on Tobacco, which was outlined briefly in Section II, progress was made toward establishing a common market in unmanufactured tobacco. It was also agreed that the Italian and French com-

[12] *European Taxation*, II/73–74, April 1971.

mercial monopolies in tobacco should be abolished. These monopolies, covering importation, manufacture and sales of tobacco and tobacco products, are clearly in contravention of Article 37 of the Treaty of Rome. So far no action has been taken but it is understood that they are to be dismantled in the near future.

On the harmonization of excise duties no agreement was forthcoming. This was a consequence not of tax differences but of differing tax structures. In particular there was difficulty in achieving a balance between the specific taxes imposed by some countries and the ad valorem taxes imposed by others. Enlargement of the Community has added to this problem, as the UK system is fundamentally different from any of the systems at present imposed in other member countries.

As far as revenue is concerned there are again quite significant differences. Italy and the UK rely much more heavily on excise duty from tobacco than do the remaining countries. As a percentage of central government revenue, duty on tobacco amounts to 8.14 per cent in the UK and 8.48 per cent in Italy. This can be compared with corresponding figures for France—2.90 per cent, Belgium—3.09 per cent and the Netherlands—3.38 per cent. In absolute terms the UK collects about 1000 million u.a. in revenue more than the next highest country which is Germany.

For two reasons comparisons of revenue may, however, be slightly misleading. Firstly, the UK system of taxing tobacco will need to be adapted to align itself with the Community's external tariff policy. Second, it is necessary to take into account differing VAT rates in the EEC countries and the proposed introduction of VAT into the UK.

The UK excise duty on tobacco is basically an import tax. With the exception of those preferences outlined in Section I duty is levied on leaf tobacco at a rate of £5.041 per lb. This is supplemented by equivalent rates for imported manufactured tobacco. From 1 January 1973 the UK is adopting, in stages covering the transitional period of membership, the EEC Common External Tariff[13]. For unmanufactured tobacco this involves an ad valorem rate of 23 per cent with fixed upper and lower limits on the amount charged.

[13] The UK and the European Communities, Cmnd 4715, HMSO, 1971.

In addition to this there is the prospect of VAT which is being introduced into the UK from April 1973. It is not certain whether this will be regarded as an additional tax or whether it will be substituted for the top segment of the present excise duty. The revenue figures given for the EEC countries are, of course, net of the VAT component. If the UK revenue figure is corrected for the two factors mentioned, to put it on a comparable basis, the overall rate of excise duty is much lower. To compare rates of excise duty, revenue is expressed in table 5 as an ad valorem rate on the basis of consumer's expenditure. This table shows that an alignment of excise duty rates will be made considerably easier if the UK value-added tax replaces part of the current excise duty[13a]. At present the overall rate of excise duty in the UK is higher than in any of the EEC countries, with the exception of Italy. The lowering of the UK duty when VAT is introduced will place it much nearer the average rate for the Community.

Table 5. Overall rates of excise duty on tobacco products, 1969

	Belgium	France	Germany	Nether.	Italy	UK
Revenue as a % of consumer expenditure	54.3	61.9	51.9	48.5	77.3	65.6[a]

Source: Statistical yearbooks of the individual countries.
UK Monthly Digest of Statistics.

Note: [a] Adjusted for common external tariff.

The introduction of ad valorem based taxes is likely to alter the structure of the tobacco market, and in particular the cigarette market, in the UK. In the past duty has been assessed on weight and moisture content, and consequently manufacturers have concentrated on small but good quality cigarettes. As more taxes are imposed on a value basis conditions will tend to favour poorer quality less expensive cigarettes and also, perhaps, larger cigarettes.

Basically the same problem, involving the balance between different types and grades of cigarettes, faces the European Commission. Its 1967 Proposal stipulated that although rates

[13a] This was the system announced in the 1973 budget, as this volume went to press.

of tax would be freely determined by each Member State, taxes must be based on retail selling price and that normally rates would be fixed as a ratio of price. This system was to be modified for cigarettes only in so far as there would be a minimum excise duty up to a certain level of retail price, and that above another determined price the pro rata duty would be replaced by a degressive scale. As can be seen from table 6 the emphasis on specific and ad valorem taxes on cigarettes varies considerably between member countries. The contrast is between, on the one hand, Germany, with a large specific tax, a lower ad valorem rate and high minimum cigarette prices, and, on the other hand, France, Belgium and the Netherlands, which rely mainly on pro rata excise duties and impose comparatively low specific taxes. The result of this situation is that good quality cigarettes are favoured in the German market, whilst cheaper cigarettes are favoured by conditions in the remaining countries[14].

Table 6. Taxation of cigarettes in the UK and EEC (u.a. per 100)

	Average selling price	Total tax element	Ad valorem rate %	Specific tax	VAT rate %
Germany	3.4	2.48	15.62	1.40	11.0
Netherlands	2.2	1.54	52.30	0.06	14.0
Belgium	1.6	1.01	55.50	(i) 0.05[a]	6.0
				(ii) 0.09	
France	1.8	1.36	Monopoly		33.3
Italy	2.2	1.70	Monopoly		12.0[b]
UK Standard					
Plain	3.7	2.76[c]	—	2.76	[d]
Standard					
Tipped	3.1	2.10	—	2,10	[d]
Small					
Plain	2.9	2.10	—	2.10	[d]
Smalled					
Tipped	2.5	1.56	—	1.56	[d]

Source: For EEC, average prices, *Der Spiegel*, quoted *Sunday Times*, August 1972.
For UK, 62nd Report Customs and Excise, Cmnd 4826.

Notes: [a] Depending on retail value.
[b] VAT rate to be introduced 1973.
[c] Imputed rate calculated by HM Customs and Excise.
[d] VAT to be introduced April 1973.

[14] The problem is further complicated by the variation in VAT rates—ranging from 6 per cent in Belgium to 33 per cent in France (table 7).

Following the rejection of the 1967 Proposal the Commission submitted, on 20 November 1970, an amended Proposal which was in turn based on a Council resolution[15]. This 1970 Proposal provided for harmonization in a number of stages and was based primarily on a 'mixed excise' system. The Commission's argument was that 'a proportional taxation system was such as to compromise the competitive position of expensive cigarettes, while a specific system has the contrary effect by putting cheap cigarettes at a disadvantage'. A mixed excise system involving 'the precise combination of the two elements' will, therefore, allow 'neutrality at the level of competition'[16]. This is a more politically acceptable formula but it does seem a rather arbitrary measure of 'neutrality' which does not apply to absolute price difference (maintained by a specific tax) or to fixed relative prices (maintained by an ad valorem tax). The adoption of mixed excise duties will ensure a regressive system over the whole price range.

A further problem has been the position of the small retailer attempting to compete with larger outlets where prices may be lower. If the taxable basis for cigarettes is the retail selling price then an ad valorem tax will gather a greater absolute amount of revenue per unit from the more expensive outlet. This may, it is argued, undermine the competitive position of the small shopkeeper. In this case neutrality of competition between the outlets has been defined by the Commission in terms of a given price difference. The taxable basis for cigarettes is not now to be the retail price but a 'fixed price', which will presumably be lower than the price charged by the small retailer.

For other tobacco products besides cigarettes the 1967 Proposal had maintained that an equal ad valorem rate should be levied in each Member State, at 20 per cent for cigars and cigarillos, 30 per cent for chewing tobacco and snuff, and 40 per cent for smoking tobacco. The 1970 Proposal was more modest in its demands. It proposed that by the end of the first stage of harmonization excise duties on cigars and cigarillos should not exceed 40 per cent and those on smoking tobacco should not exceed 50 per cent. It was suggested that chewing

[15] *European Bulletin* 1/1971.
[16] *European Taxation* II/153.

tobacco and snuff should be exempt from all excise duties.

These rates apply mainly to those countries where at present monopolies exist, i.e. France and Italy. In the other EEC countries, with the exception of the UK, current rates are far below those suggested by the Commission's report. In Germany the ad valorem rate on cigars is 18.58 per cent; in the Netherlands there are two rates—8.43 per cent and 14.43 per cent—depending on weight; and in Belgium there are again two rates—11.5 per cent and 16.0 per cent. In the UK, of course, there is the standard specific tax levied on cigars and smoking tobacco at £5.041 per lb.

Beer, Wines and Spirits

Of the taxes considered, the variation in national tax rates is most pronounced in the case of duties levied on beers, wines and spirits. In particular it is clear that duty rates in the UK are higher than comparable rates in the rest of the Community. In part this discrepancy between Member States is reflected in the revenue figures given previously in table 2. Receipts from duties imposed on beer, wines and spirits average between 2 and 3 per cent of central government revenue in the original six EEC countries, whilst in the UK the corresponding figure is over 6 per cent[17].

We shall begin this section by considering excise duties levied on beer. Taxation of beer in the UK is traditionally relied upon to provide a large proportion (currently something over 3 per cent) of central government revenue. In no other EEC country is the tax so important from a revenue point of view. This is the case even though per capita consumption of beer is higher in both Germany and Belgium. To gain an initial idea of the divergence between national rates of duty implicit tax rates have been calculated based on the amount of tax paid and the volume of beer consumed. These implicit rates are shown in table 7. It was necessary to calculate duty rates in this way, as differences in tax structures tend to make direct comparisons impossible. This aspect is discussed in more detail below.

[17] The relevant figures are: Belgium 2.16 per cent, France 1.91 per cent, Germany 2.70 per cent, Italy 1.05 per cent, Netherlands 2.33 per cent and the UK 6.10 per cent.

Table 7. Implicit rates of duty on beer according to consumption, 1969 (u.a. per hectolitre)

Belgium	France	Germany	Italy	Nether.	UK
4.01	1.32	3.83	7.21	5.63	19.73

Source: As for table 5.

According to the method of calculation adopted the average duty on beer in the original EEC countries is 3.72 u.a. per hectolitre[18] compared with 19.73 u.a./hl. which is the corresponding figure for the UK. These figures do not take account, however, of differences in VAT and sales taxes. Nor do they reflect the fact that duty is usually calculated not only on volume consumed but also on the strength or proof content of the beer.

Allowing for these factors does not change the main conclusion that an equalization of duty rates throughout the Community will be extremely difficult if not impossible. The Commission in its 1972 Proposal does not consider this problem. It confines itself to the prior problem of deciding on a common structure of beer taxation. Basically there are two methods of assessing duty. The first system, which is currently used in the Benelux countries, Italy and the UK, is to calculate the amount of tax on the basis of the worts—this is the liquid produced from the mash before the process of fermentation has begun. The alternative method, which has been adopted in W. Germany and France, is to base the amount of tax on the alcoholic strength of the final beer.

The problem for the Commission in its 1972 Proposal was to decide at what stage in the production process the harmonized duty on beer should be levied. The UK system, which is typical of the one alternative, was adopted long ago in the Inland Revenue Act, 1880. It was decided then that duty should be charged according to the quantity and the specific gravity of the worts produced. Specific gravity is used because the brewing value of the worts depends on the extract value, i.e. the excess weight over the weight of an equal volume of water. If the weight of water is then represented by 1000 the duty will vary with the number of degrees in excess of 1000. This means that

[18] Weighted average according to 1969 consumption figures.

whatever the dilution or contraction the charge on the worts is the same and thus duty will vary approximately with the strength of the beer. In the UK there is a standard charge of £10.375 per barrel (36 gallons) at 1030 degrees plus £0.44 for each additional degree. The levying of duty is primarily on brewer's accounts but this is supplemented by sample checks at breweries.

Similar systems are applied in Italy and the Benelux countries. In Italy, where duty is highest except for the UK, tax officials keep a permanent check on breweries. Duty is charged at 4 lire per litre per degree of sweetness of the wort. In the Benelux countries the position is slightly more complicated, as the duty rate depends not only on properties of the extract or essence but also on the annual output of the individual brewery. A progressive scale of taxes is used, and gives a competitive advantage to the smaller breweries. To some extent, however, this advantage may be cancelled by regulations concerning losses sustained in the production process. In the UK a deduction of 6 per cent is made from the assessment 'to allow for subsequent wastage and loss during the preparation of the beer for consumption'. In Italy a deduction of 14 per cent is made to cover these losses. But in the Benelux countries production loss is not taken into account, and hence an advantage is given to the more efficient breweries.

The European Commission in its 1972 Proposal has come out against the system of beer taxation based on worts. It advises that the systems outlined above should be replaced by taxes based on the strength of the final beer, i.e. with the system currently based in Germany and recently adopted for France. The Commission favours this second system for a number of reasons.

Firstly, because a system not based on the final product encounters some difficulty in dealing appropriately with imports. Strictly speaking it is necessary to calculate the original quantity and quality of the worts used, and as this is not possible some arbitrary ruling must be made. For instance, in the Benelux countries a standard percentage is added to imports to cover original production losses. Similarly, it may be difficult accurately to calculate rebates for export. With the second method of assessment it is possible to tax imports and domestic production on the same basis.

Secondly, as explained above, the duty calculated on the worts is not entirely independent of conditions of production. There are losses involved in the production process and according to the Commission's report these can vary between 6 per cent and 25 per cent depending on the efficiency of the brewery. A standard loss clause will tend to favour the more efficient brewery.

Finally, it is possible to impose taxes based on a commercial classification of beer. This is already done in Germany and in fact the classification proposed by the Commission follows the German classification quite closely:

Class		*Percentage by weight of Original Extract* *German Classification*	*EEC Classification*
III	Small or simple beer	2%— 5%	1%— 4%
II	Medium of draught beer	7%— 8%	7%— 9.5%
I	Strong of full beer	11%—14%	11%—13.5%
S	Extra strong beer	16%+	15.5+

The amount of duty charged in Germany depends on the output of the particular brewery. However, the duty on medium or draught beer is approximately 0.7p per pint. A correspondingly approximate imputed figure for the UK is 4.7p per pint.

In France an excise tax on beer was introduced in the 1969 Finance Act. Duty is assessed there in two classes according to the alcoholic strength of the beer. Firstly, beer with alcoholic strength not exceeding 4.6 degrees or beer put into containers with capacity of less than 1 litre is charged at 4.5 F/hl. All remaining beer is charged at 8.0 F/hl. In comparison not only with the UK but also with other member countries the French excise duty is low. Even the upper rate implies a charge of less than 0.4p/pint.

As with the other taxes considered it can be misleading to compare excise duties without bearing in mind the different levels of VAT imposed in the different countries. In the UK a value-added tax came into force in April 1973 which replaces part of the existing excise duty. Clearly it eases one of the problems of harmonization if current rates of duty are lowered, as it is announced that they will be. VAT rates in the remaining countries are given in table 8.

Table 8. Rates of VAT on beer in the EEC, 1972

France	Netherlands	Belgium	Germany	Italy
17.6%	14.0%	6.0%	11.0%	7.0%[a]

[a] Rate of general turnover tax.

The 1972 Proposal does not deal with the problem of aligning absolute rates of excise duty. However, it does attempt to specify the relative amount of duty to be charged on each class of beer. Again it follows most closely the present German system. The report recommends that class II (medium or draught beer) should be taxed at 70 per cent of the rate imposed on class I (strong beer); that class III (small beer) should be taxed at 30 per cent of the class I rate; and that extra strong beer should be taxed at 150 per cent of the rate on strong beer. The current German rates are: class II=75 per cent class I; class III =50 per cent class I; and class S=150 per cent class I[19]. It seems, therefore, that the EEC proposals on beer require only marginal changes to be made in the German system, whilst in the UK, Italy and the Benelux countries quite large changes would have to be made in adopting a new structure of beer taxation.

The difficulties facing the Commission regarding the taxation of wine were more fundamental than those for beer. This stemmed from the fact that excise duties on wine did not exist in all the Member States. The question, therefore, was whether existing taxes should be abolished or whether they should be generalized throughout the Community. The 1972 Proposal recommends that duty on wine should be introduced in Italy, where no excise duties are levied on wine, and also in Germany, where currently there is only duty charged on sparkling wine.

The Commission supported this recommendation with a number of arguments. It claimed, for instance, that beer and wine were in close competition in some Member States and that

[19] In the initial stages of harmonization this structure of rates would not rule out special provision being made for brewery size in Germany and the Benelux countries. The necessity of a constant factor between tax rates does not rule out a progressive scale according to output but ultimately this will be abolished.

if beer was to be subject to a system of harmonized excise duties then a duty should also be levied on wine, lest it gain a competitive advantage over beer. But this did not mean that beer and wine should be taxed at the same rate, and the proposal failed to explain how a competitive differential in tax should be arrived at. The Commission also argued that certain products, including wine and spirits, should be taxed up to their 'contributive capacity' and that this was difficult to achieve if reliance was placed solely on a value-added tax with a limited number of rates. An excise duty on wine would allow more flexibility in this respect and, moreover, would not be administratively difficult to impose. In the EEC countries a system of checks and controls already operate as part of the common organization of the market in vine products[20].

The main point made in the proposal was that the revenue currently obtained from duties on wine was thought sufficiently important to rule out the possibility of abolition. The proposal did not, of course, directly consider the UK but the point is even more valid in this context. Although per capita consumption of wine in the UK is low, high rates of tax mean that duties yield over twice as much revenue as do those in France (table 2).

The UK system of taxing wine has already been outlined in Section I. The basic division is into still wines and sparkling wines and these are further subdivided into heavy wines and light wines. For each category there are a number of rates depending on the origin of the wine. The lowest applies to domestic production, the highest to imports which come from neither the Commonwealth nor EFTA. The subdivision between heavy and light wines also depends on the origin of the wine. It may be 25 degrees proof or 27 degrees proof. For purposes of comparison we shall henceforth express this in terms of degrees Gay Lussac[21]. The lower division corresponds to 14.3° GL, the upper to 15.4° GL. This division between heavy and light wines coincides approximately with one adopted in the Commission's 1972 Proposal.

The Proposal begins by considering a definition of the taxable product. Under the category of wine it wishes to include products 'obtained exclusively by alcoholic fermentation of

---

[20] For background see *European Bulletin* 11/1969.
[21] 4° GL (Gay Lussac) = 7° proof.

fresh grapes or the musts of fresh grapes' which have 'a total maximum strength of 15° GL'. There are certain exceptions to the second part of the definition in so far as wines of a strength greater than 15° GL may be taxed as wine if they are produced in specified regions of the Community. Other wines, including aperitifs and liqueur wines and much of what is now categorized in the UK as heavy wine, will come under the proposed harmonized structure for taxes on alcohol dealt with below.

The system proposed for wine is similar to that operating in France, where there is one fiscal regime for wines with a strength below 15° GL and another, based on the tax on alcohol, for wines in excess of 15° GL. The French system differs from the tax structures in the remaining countries. In the Benelux countries excise duties on wine have already been harmonized and tax rates have been aligned. The system there is based on three classes—sparkling wines, still wines with a strength of up to 22° GL and wine with a strength over 22° GL. This is supplemented by a surcharge on extra alcohol if the wine is stronger than 12° GL. In Italy, although there is no excise duty on wine as such, there is again a surcharge on alcohol if the wine is stronger than 12° GL.

The differing tax structures tend to confuse any straightforward comparison of tax rates. Even so, table 9 below

Table 9. Rates of excise duty on wines in EEC and UK (u.a. per hectolitre)

	France	Benelux	Italy	UK[a]
Sparkling wine	1.62[b] 4.05	42.0	14.4% (IGE)	94.0 107.0
Non-sparkling wine				
12° GL	1.62[c] 4.05	12.0	—	78.5
12–15° GL	1.62 4.05	12.0–18.3	1.44–4.32[d]	78.5
15° GL+	[e]	22.2+3.4 per add.°	4.32+1.44 per add.°	91.7
VAT rates	17.6%	14.0%	12.0%	—

Notes: [a] Division between heavy and light wines.
[b] Higher rate applies to champagne; the lower rate to other sparkling wine.
[c] Higher rate applies to sweet natural wine; the lower rate to other wine.
[d] Tax on excess alcohol over 12° GL.
[e] Wines in excess of 15° GL are taxed under the rates for alcohol.

illustrates how far out of line are duty rates in the UK. Because the future of preferential margins is uncertain the figures quoted pertain to the rate levied on domestic production, i.e. the lowest rate. This is, nevertheless, far in excess of the corresponding rates for the Benelux countries and France. The rates in France are particularly low, as is the surcharge imposed on alcoholic content in Italy. The rate charged on sparkling wine in the Benelux countries is surprisingly high but even this is less than half the UK rate.

In much the same way as with wine and beer the UK excise duty on alcohol diverges considerably from the level of taxation adopted in the rest of the Community. In each Member State there is a tax imposed on ethyl alcohol (C_2H_5OH). Usually this tax is levied at a number of different rates depending primarily on the category of use.

The highest rate is generally applied to alcohol used in the manufacture of wines and beverages and this is the main source of revenue. The relevant rates are shown in table 10. The UK excise duty on alcoholic spirit is over twice the average rate for the rest of the Community. The approximate tax in the UK on a bottle of Scotch whisky (70° proof) is £2.20. The same rate of duty applies to Commonwealth rum and Irish whisky.

Table 10. Rates of tax on spirits used for alcoholic beverages. (u.a. per hectolitre of absolute alcohol)

	Belgium	Germany	Nether.	Italy	UK
Excise duty	440.0	409.8	469.6	222.0	995.2
VAT	25%	11%	14%	4%	—

The system of taxation in Italy is based partly on how the spirit is produced. The total tax element is divided in two parts; a manufacturing tax and a state tax. The state tax varies inversely with the cost of the raw material used. Thus for alcohol produced from cereal (a relatively cheap method) there is a standard rate which is reduced if the alcohol is derived from other products such as molasses, sugar cane, locust beans, figs, dates, dried grapes, etc. The 1972 Proposal recommends that this basis for taxation be abolished.

In France, which is not included in table 10, there are two taxes—a consumption tax and a fabrication tax—with rates which depend on the type of beverage produced. Under the consumption tax, rum is charged at a lower rate than other spirits. Under the fabrication tax both aperitifs (based on wine) and gin are taxed at a lower rate. The Commission's Proposal suggests that rates of excise duty for alcohol contained in aromatized wines and liqueur wines should be taxed at less than the full rate. The full list of current rates in France is as follows:

	u.a./hl. of absolute alcohol
Consumption Tax	
Vermouth and other aromatic wines	414.0
Spirits for the manufacture of beverages	
(a) Rum and Creme de cassis	334.8
(b) other	414.0
Fabrication Tax	
Alcoholic drinks derived from cereals (except Gin)	207.0
Aperitifs other than those based on wine	207.0
Aperitifs based on wine and vermouths	70.2
Gin	70.2

Aside from the taxation of alcoholic beverages rebates are generally allowed on other uses. In the UK, for instance, there is a rebate on spirits used for medical and scientific purposes. The rebate allowed is the duty paid in excess of the equivalent duty in force in 1918. A similar rebate for medicaments is allowed in other countries.

In all the countries there are either reduced rates or exemptions for spirits rendered non-potable by methylation. In the UK methylated spirits used for domestic purposes or industrial purposes are duty free. In many of the EEC countries a reduced tax is also allowed on spirits used in the manufacture of perfumes, cosmetics and toilet articles. The 1972 Proposal recommends that these spirits as well as those used for external medical purposes should be exempt from the payment of duty.

IV. SOME PRICE, REVENUE AND DISTRIBUTIONAL EFFECTS OF THE HARMONIZATION OF EXCISE DUTIES

As suggested by the format of this chapter the harmonization of excise duties can be looked at in two or three stages.

The first stage covers those changes necessitated by membership and arising out of the introduction of VAT, the introduction of the Common External Tariff, and the abolition of domestic and Commonwealth preferences. The price and revenue effects of this stage depend to some extent on future government policy. It may be that rates of excise duty will remain unaltered with the introduction of value-added tax and the Community tariff, in which case there will be corresponding price rises in excisable products with the exception of petrol. But more likely there will be some substitution of taxes, and in this case there may well be no price effect but a corresponding fall in excise duty revenue. As for domestic and Commonwealth preferences the margins involved are small, and therefore the price effects consequent upon their abolition are also likely to be small. Some effect may be noticeable with tobacco, as the preference margin (about $1\frac{1}{2}$ per cent off the standard rate) applies to over half of total imports, but the effect of abolishing the surcharges on beer and spirits is likely to be negligible. With wine, elimination of the domestic preference could seriously affect the competitive position of British wine but otherwise would have little effect on overall prices.

The second and third stages of harmonization cover structural harmonization and the eventual alignment of national rates of excise duty. As we have seen throughout the previous section, many of the main issues have been raised by the 1972 Proposal but no agreement has yet been possible concerning the details of the second stage. This means in turn, of course, that actual enforced changes in duty rates may be some way off in the future. But, even taking this into account, it may be useful in this final section to look briefly at the approximate magnitudes of changes required in the third stage of harmonization and attempt to assess some possible effects of movements toward a harmonized system of excise rates throughout the Community.

Turning first of all to the duty on mineral oils, it is here that the UK rates of excise duty correspond closest to those in the remaining member countries. This is illustrated in table 4 which shows tax rates on petroleum in the UK and the EEC. In terms of total tax (VAT plus excise duties) the UK rate approximates to that charged in the Netherlands and in Germany: these countries having the lowest tax rates of those considered. But, as we have stressed previously, the harmonization of excise duties must be viewed in the context of an alignment of VAT rates. With the exception of the UK, 'mixed' excise systems operate in the EEC and the final harmonized level will almost certainly be expressed in terms of a given specific element and a given ad valorem element.

To proceed to some sort of average position within the Community the total tax burden on petroleum in the UK will be increased. The amount of this increase is uncertain but is likely to be in the region of 4p per gallon. This is a relatively large increase and will, of course, have revenue consequences. Simply by taking current consumption levels such an increase means that tax receipts from this source will be swelled by up to £170 million.

But it would be wrong to think of this as increased revenue from excise duties. The specific duty imposed in the UK is already higher than in other countries with the exception of Italy. If anything, the specific part of the tax in the UK should be reduced or held constant. The major changes required consist in the alignment of value-added tax rates and any increase should come in this form.

With regard to specific taxes on fuel oils (see table 5) the Commission plan for a 2 u.a./m. ton on heavy fuel oils and a 5 u.a./m. ton tax on light fuel oils implies price reductions throughout the Community except for France which already conforms with this system. In the UK acceptance of such a plan could entail a revenue loss of perhaps £40–50 million. But, as we have seen, the Commission plan has attracted criticism with respect to both the level of rates and to the balance between heavy and light fuels. An average of current rates in the Community would considerably reduce the anticipated revenue losses associated with the Commission's Proposal.

When we turn from the price and revenue consequences to the distributional aspects of harmonization a whole host of new difficulties arise. Some stem from the necessarily rather tentative nature of price effects; others concern the basic methodology of measuring the impact of tax changes on income distribution. As in the previous chapter, data from the UK annual Family Expenditure Survey has been used, along with results obtained on the incidence of taxes and social service benefits[22]. The inherent difficulties associated with this method are well accounted for elsewhere[23] and it suffices to mention here that the sample may not exhibit the same characteristics as the overall population; that the accuracy of returns for some categories of expenditure (notably tobacco and alcoholic drink) is somewhat dubious; and that the demand assumptions make the calculations more relevant to marginal changes than to large changes in tax rates.

Bearing these factors in mind it is clear that detailed conclusions should be viewed with a healthy suspicion although it is possible by use of this method to bring out the main tendencies relevant to a given tax change. Further difficulties are met, however, in framing a useful hypothesis concerning the nature of the tax change. Generally speaking an equi-revenue change is required in which case the regressivity/progressivity of the main tax can be obscured by the effect of the tax it is to replace or be replaced by. In considering the distributional effects of changes in excise duties revenue gains and losses have been compensated for by means of a proportional tax on original income. This serves to highlight the actual effects of changes in the excise duties themselves, though the results will have to be modified if, for instance, reductions in excise duties are compensated for by increases in VAT.

In the case of mineral oils, as made plain above, the change in total tax will fall upon the value-added tax component rather than the excise duty. However, as an illustration, we have included the distributional effects of this change in table 11. The hypothesized change involves an increase in the tax on petroleum by one fifth, the revenue consequences of this being compensated for by a proportional tax/subsidy based on original income (i.e. income before direct taxes and benefits). As can be seen from table 11 the net effects of such a change are very small and no consistent pattern can be detected in the income group classification. Whilst the increase in tax burden

[22] CSO Family Expenditure Survey 1970: 'The incidence of taxes and social service benefits in 1970', *Economic Trends*, No. 220, February 1972.

[23] See previous chapter, pp. 39–53, and C. V. Brown, 'Impact of tax changes on income distribution', PEP Institute for Fiscal Studies, Broadsheet 525.

Table 11. Net distributional effects of hypothesized changes in excise duties.[a]

Percentage changes in average incomes after direct taxes and benefits.[b]

Original Income Range (£)	Under 260	260–	315–	382–	460–	559–	676–	816–	988–	1196–	1448–	1752–	2122–	2566–	3104–
All households															
Tobacco	+0.43	+0.48	+0.36	+0.30	+0.37	+0.21	+0.30	+0.32	+0.24	+0.16	+0.09	—	−0.08	−0.11	−0.30
Drink	+0.35	+0.44	+0.13	+0.10	+0.14	−0.25	+0.11	+0.11	−0.02	−0.02	−0.06	−0.01	−0.09	−0.01	−0.03
Oil	+0.07	+0.01	−0.05	—	+0.02	−0.05	—	−0.04	+0.07	+0.01	+0.05	+0.01	−0.02	+0.02	−0.09

Source: The Incidence of taxes and social service benefits in 1970. *Economic Trends*, No. 220 February 1972.

Notes: [a] Hypothesized changes of 15% cut in tobacco tax, 20% increase in oil tax, and 30% cut in taxes on drink.
[b] For definitions and survey details see source material and Family Expenditure Survey for 1970.

is well spread it does appear that the main beneficiaries are those in the top income bracket.

Going on to tobacco the picture is somewhat different. Assuming again some form of Community average as the most likely solution for the harmonized level, both the prices of tobacco goods in the UK and the revenue obtained from excise duties on tobacco will be reduced. As pointed out in section III of this chapter price effects must take into account VAT and the introduction of the Common External Tariff. Even then the overall price effect will be misleading in so far as structural alterations to the tax (converting it into a 'mixed' excise system) will radically alter price differentials in the tobacco market. This is shown quite clearly in table 12 which is an attempt to estimate the effect on UK cigarette prices of adopting the various excise systems current in other member countries. In modifying the basis of assessment from weight to value the largest price reductions are in the larger, and untipped, cigarettes. Further, the price reductions are larger under the Benelux systems than under the systems current in W. Germay and France[24]. The overall price and revenue effects will therefore depend on quite complicated demand and supply responses.

Table 12. Estimated effect on UK cigarette prices as a result of adopting EEC excise systems.

(percentages)

	W. Germany	Nether.	Belgium	France
Excise duties only				
Standard plain	−27.0	−58.8	−56.7	−31.4
Small plain	−12.3	−54.8	−52.3	−25.5
Standard tipped	−10.5	−47.9	−45.3	−12.9
Small tipped	+ 8.2	−39.1	−35.9	+ 1.6

Note: See table 5.

Taking as a guide a 15 per cent reduction in duty there would be an estimated revenue loss of perhaps £200 million and this, as can be seen from the table above, would still leave the UK level of duty above the Community average. The distributional effects of a change of this magnitude are described in table 11. From the example given, the regressive nature of the tobacco

[24] In France, aside from there being a monopoly system, value-added tax is levied at 33.3 per cent.

tax is made clear. Compensating again by means of a proportional income tax there is a seemingly straightforward transfer away from households with an original income in excess of £1750 per annum. However, as a cautionary note, the pattern is not so clearcut if more detailed figures are used, with a breakdown into family types and pensioners. These latter figures do tend to suggest that one-adult households in the middle income ranges, for example, fare relatively badly as a result of the change.

Finally we turn to the effects of harmonizing duties on beer, wines and spirits. In each of these cases there are wide differences between the Community average and the current rate in the UK. For beer a new system of taxation has been put forward in the Commission's 1972 Proposal. This, if accepted, would have the effect of changing existing price differentials between different types and strengths of beer. But the adoption of Community rates presents a more fundamental change. Taking the 1971 average price of 12p per pint of beer in the UK, this included duty paid of approximately 4.7p. This can be compared (see table 13 below) with corresponding EEC rates of between 0.3p (France) and 1.7p (Italy). To attain a Community average the UK duty would need to be effectively reduced by between 3p and 4p. Such a course of action, although it would stimulate consumption, would clearly lead to a significant reduction in revenue. Even a reduction of 50 per cent implies a loss of revenue in excess of £200 million.

The situation concerning the harmonization of duties on spirits can be characterized in much the same way. The diver-

Table 13. Estimated duty effects on beer and spirits of adopting EEC Excise duties

Retail price in UK	Present duty payable in UK	Estimated duty payable in EEC: Italy	Ger.	France	Bel.	Nether.
Scotch Whisky[a]						
£2.47½ to £3.07½	£2.20	£0.49	£0.86	£0.46	£0.97	£1.03
Beer[b]						
12p per pint	4.7p	1.7p	0.9p	0.3p	0.9p	1,3p

Notes: [a] Scotch Whisky, 1971, 26⅔ oz. bottle, 70° proof.
[b] Beer, 1971, assumed strength of 1.037°. See 62nd Report of Customs and Excise, Cmd. 4826.

gence between duty rates in the UK and the rest of the Community can be illustrated with regard to the cost of whisky. The calculated duty on a bottle of Scotch whisky in the UK is £2.20, which can be compared with corresponding EEC rates in the range £0.46 (France) to £1.03 (Netherlands). Again a reduction in duty of 50 per cent would still leave the UK rate above the average in the rest of the Community, and yet mean a substantial revenue loss of over £150 million.

Finally, as we have seen earlier, the differences in national rates of duty on wine are so pronounced that it seems presumptuous to think at all in terms of a harmonized level (see table 9). However, it should be noted that a reduction or even abolition of the UK duty on wine would not cause revenue difficulties of the order associated with the changes envisaged for beer, spirits and tobacco. An overall figure must, of course, be approximate but it seems likely that a programme of equalizing excise duties would lead to a shortfall in UK revenue of something in excess of £650 million.

Whether this revenue loss is thought to be prohibitive or whether the revenue can be made up, for instance by raising rates of value-added tax, is a matter for future policy. The purpose of this paper has been simply to highlight the main difficulties involved in accepting the objective of harmonizing and equalizing excise duties. To date, the EEC Proposals have concentrated on structural harmonization alone. And even here the technical difficulties are formidable. But, more important, the harmonization of structures is seen as a preliminary to the eventual equalization of nominal rates and this would imply repercussions on income distribution, particularly noting the present regressivity of taxes on tobacco and alcoholic drink, and, more significantly, repercussions on the structure of tax revenues in the UK.

4

The Corporation Tax

by Douglas Dosser

THE position regarding the corporation tax is curious and confusing. As will be well known, Britain is currently in process of changing from the system introduced by a Labour Government in 1965, substantially back to the system which existed prior to that date[1]. This follows consideration of the issue by a Select Committee of the House of Commons[2].

This British situation needs to be viewed against the background of Community developments on the corporation tax, since it is a tax eventually due for harmonization.

On the Continent, the present situation is equally fluid. For example, the French have the system to which the British are changing. The Germans have a different system again, although plans to change to the Franco-British system have been under intense discussion and have been an important political issue. But other Member States have a system corresponding to the present British system.

This spate of re-thinking and change has not involved a nice convergence—spontaneous harmonization—to Community norms as envisaged by the Commission. The report of the Committee[3] set up by the Commission to study the matter on its economic merits came out in favour of the British 1965 system, which, as mentioned, is currently being abandoned by Britain.

In spite of the opposed positions of the Tempel Report and the existing French/proposed British/ possible German system,

[1] See Report on the Corporation Tax, Cmnd 4630, March 1971 (Green Paper) and ditto, Cmnd 4955, April 1972 (White Paper), HMSO, Finance Act, 1972, and Budget statement 1973.

[2] Report of the Select Committee on the Corporation Tax, October 1971.

[3] EEC Corporation Tax and Individual Tax (the Tempel Report), Brussels, 1970.

it is expected that the Commission will press forward with the recommendations made in the Tempel Report.

What the eventual outcome will be for a harmonized Community system it is impossible to predict at present. This puts this chapter on the corporation tax into singular difficulties. It is too early to consider economic consequences of plausible alternatives when the outcome of the Community/Member State clash on the basic system might well result in a muddy compromise or a very long delay in evolving a common system.

We begin, in the following section, with a comparison of the three basic current systems of corporation taxes, so that the issues between the Community and the Member States can be more clearly understood.

Comparative Evaluation of Current Systems[4]

There are three main schemes of Corporation Tax to be considered:

(1) Complete Separation of Corporation and Personal Income Tax (to be called the Separate System).

This is the present British system, and represents System A in the Tempel Report. It is often also called the 'Classical' system.

(2) The Split Rate System or Two-Rate System (to be called the Two-Rate System).

The present German system, and System B in the Tempel Report and also the main alternative system suggested for UK in the Green Paper.

(3) The Credit or Imputation System (to be called the Credit System).

The present French system, and System C in the Tempel Report, and the proposed system for UK in the White Paper.

In evaluating one system against another, on economic grounds, there are domestic factors, and international factors to be taken into consideration.

This section indicates the path of such an evaluation in outline only. For the effect of the corporation tax, in its various forms, on economic factors in the domestic and international

---

[4] Based on the author's submission to the Select Committee on the Corporation Tax, see note 2 above.

field is largely the subject of a priori statements rather than econometric work. And in the few cases where the latter has been attempted, the results are in dispute.

Domestic Factors in an Economic Evaluation

The standard list of criteria by which a tax change may be judged includes: effects on the budget revenues; income distribution; the balance of payments; growth rate; and regional effects. The effect on prices has not been specifically mentioned, but works into several of the factors listed, for example, the income distribution and the balance of payments.

Let us look briefly at each of these criteria in turn.

(i) Revenues

For the UK the revenues from the corporation tax are not so important as the other two harmonizable areas of taxation: they are much less than excise revenues and, of course, very substantially less than the potential yield of VAT.

Of course, there are significant revenue implications in the choice between the three systems. Indeed, the motivation for the present UK reforms is partly to lighten the overall tax load on business. However, this aspect is not at all a decisive one in the choice between the systems. For the same effect, namely reducing the tax-take from business, could be achieved by retention of the Separate or Classical system and lowering present rates. Since the *rate* for a Community system is an even more far-off question than the structure, this is an open question and a relatively low rate is quite feasible.

Thus, the revenue aspect of the comparison between the three systems can be neutralized by thinking in terms of a Credit or Two-Rate system with rates of corporation tax similar to those current, or a Separate system with a lower rate. Then the comparison of some of the economic merits of each structure can be more clearly made, without the somewhat confusing issue of whether one or other brings in more tax revenue.

(ii) Income Distribution

The effect on the income distribution of a corporation tax depends on both the net money receipts side of an individual's personal budget, and on the prices of consumer goods facing him.

The effect on the money receipts side depends on the comparative size of dividends paid out, and the tax taken from them.

Now one of the main arguments for the 1965 UK reform, introducing the Separate system, was the encouragement of retentions. We might assume that such use of corporate profits promoting investment and growth was to the benefit of the community at large. Therefore, the Two-Rate and Credit systems, with higher pay-out ratios of cash to shareholders, who are assumed to be mainly in the top-half of the income bracket scale, might tend to be regressive in its distributional effect. Further, this is reinforced by the fact that a lower proportion of dividend receipts has to be paid away in tax under the Two-Rate and Credit systems, taking the Corporate Tax and Personal Tax liability together. (Although this last effect disappears in a strictly equal-revenue comparison, this would require a reduced rate under the Separate system compared to that current.)

This is not quite the end of the distribution story. The main econometric thrust of recent years on the corporation tax has been an attempt to answer the question: is the corporation tax raised on the company really paid out of profits, as traditional economic theory has held, or does the company recoup the tax by raising product prices?[5]

If the tax raised on the company is 'passed forward', this makes the incidence of the corporation tax, of whatever type, fall on the consumer: more or less corporation tax nominally paid by a company implies a greater or smaller 'expenditure' or 'sales' tax, progressive or regressive according to the alternative means of raising the same revenue. Only if at least some of the tax is not passed forward do we get the regressive tendency of the Two-Rate and Credit systems.

Since the 'complete forward shifting' hypothesis has been heavily criticized, the pointers are to regressive distributional effects of a change from the present system to the two alternatives.

[5] M. Krzyzaniak and R. A. Musgrave, *The Shifting of the Corporation Income Tax*, Johns Hopkins Press, 1963, and M. Krzyzaniak (ed.), *Effects of Corporation Income Tax*, Wayne State University Press, 1966.

But this is an example of the a priori reasoning noted earlier. No statistical study of these income effects is available for the corporation tax, similar to those now becoming available for the introduction of the value-added tax.

Our own distributional remarks have concentrated on the current income effects of the alternate systems on the shareholder. The more usual argument is in terms of wealth effects, namely the effects on prices of shares held. It is usually asserted that the UK 1965 system is depressive of share prices, the alternatives encouraging. The arguments about share prices have been well-worked over by others, and will not be pursued here.

In so far as they are true, they again work in the same direction —the alternatives are regressive in income and wealth aspects.

(*iii*) *Balance of Payments*

The question of the effects of the alternative systems has to be considered under the current and capital sides of the balance of payments. Discussion of the capital aspects is, of course, closely connected with the international aspects of corporation tax reform which will be dealt with later.

The main current account lies in exports. As regards shorter-run price effects, rather than longer-run growth effects, to be considered later, several analytical points made under the preceding distributional section affect the issue—the proportion of total tax paid by the corporation compared with the individual shareholder, and the degree to which the corporation's liability can be passed forward.

If the tax is not passed forward, the fact that the Separate system leaves a greater proportion of profits in the hands of the company could imply that it can sell at keener prices in international markets. The compensating difference in shareholder receipts does not have the same potential effect on prices. If the corporation tax is passed forward, then of course the total tax to be paid by the consumers in the Separate system (unless the Separate system rate is reduced) may exceed that under the Two-Rate system, as shown in table 1. If export prices are involved here, the Separate system could have adverse price effects on exports. However, it might be argued that passing forward may be possible in home markets, whilst not possible in export markets due to keener market competition.

The short-run effect on the current balance of payments is thus equivocal, and dependent on many factors. But there is also a long-run effect on exports, which will form part of our discussion of growth. And effects on the capital account may outweigh all of these current account effects.

(*iv*) *Growth*

Taking a simple causal relation between a higher rate of investment and the rate of growth, the most important economic argument for the 1965 system is to be found here. The Separate system certainly leaves a higher proportion of earnings, after tax and distribution, in the company's hands for re-investment. The growth rate particularly in manufacturing industry ought to be raised, and therefore exports especially benefited.

Table 1. Comparison of separate and two-rate systems

1. Assumptions

Two-Rate System as in Green Paper[2]
50% and 20%, 30% rate of income tax.

Equal Yield Separate Tax
38%; 30% rate of income tax.

2. Allocation of tax charges

	Separate	Two-Rate
Corporate Earnings	100	100
Payout Ratio	40/60	60/40
Corporation Tax	38%=100=38	50%×40=20 20%×60=$\frac{12}{32}$
Income Tax	30% on 40=12	30% on 60=18
Total Tax	50	50
Tax on Retentions	38%×60=22.8	50%×40=20
Tax on Distributions	(38%+30%)×40=27.2	(20%+30%)×60=30

3. Allocation of corporate earnings

3.1. Corporate tax *not* passed forward

	Earnings	Corporation	Shareholders	Government
Separate	100	60−22.8 =37.2[1]	40−27.2 +12.8[2]	50[1]
Two-Rate	100	40−20 =20[1]	60−30 =30[2]	50[1]

3.2. Corporate tax passed forward 100%

	Earnings	Corporation	Consumers	Shareholders	Government
Separate	100	60[1]	−22.8[3]	12.8[2]	50[1]
Two-Rate	100	40[1]	−20.0[3]	30.0[2]	50[1]

[1] general benefit
[2] benefit to higher income groups
[3] general burden

This position is countered by (a) the empirical claim that our investment record has been poor since 1965, (b) the a priori argument that even if investment is increased it is not necessarily being used in the most productive uses, which would be achieved by distribution through the competitive market in investible funds, but just 'used up' in low-productivity ways in old-established and possibly declining industries[6].

These are a priori grounds for claiming the Separate system is good for growth. But the increase in investment from retentions may be of low quality.

Like all of these domestic economic factors, comparison between the systems is marked by a lack of empirical evidence. On a priori grounds, much seems to favour the Separate system.

International Factors in an Economic Evaluation

As is well known, the Tempel Report[7] favours the Separate system, because it is 'neutral' in its tax treatment between domestic investments at home and overseas, and between domestic and foreign investment at home (provided the foreign government is also following the same system).

If each Member State of an economic community is following the Separate system, the country of source of earnings from the investment takes the proceeds of the corporation tax plus a withholding against personal income tax liability, while the country of residence of the shareholder raises the personal income tax granting credit for the withholding.

So once the corporation tax is harmonized, say at 50 per cent, and also the withholding rate, say at 15 per cent, a British

[6] See J. Chown, *The Reform of Corporation Tax*, Institute for Fiscal Studies, March 1971.
[7] See note 3.

investor in Britain and in another Member State will pay 65 per cent on income earned from whatever source, plus income tax. The tax payment of a resident of a Member State will thus initially be equal. But personal income tax liability will vary according to the different personal tax rate systems of the countries concerned. But this will not effect the choice between investments of the resident of any state because the same personal tax schedule will apply to all investments.

Thus the Separate system (with harmonization of the corporation tax and withholding) allows complete non-discrimination between domestic and other Member State investment, consonant with national differences in choice of personal income tax schedules.

If the Separate system exists without harmonization, as would be the case even between Member States of an economic community and some non-members, non-discrimination exists between domestic and foreign investent at home, but not necessarily between investment inside and outside the Community by a particular national (unless specifically arranged through a tax treaty). Nor is there reciprocity in the total corporation tax and withholding paid by any two nationals with investments in each other's country (unless specifically arranged through a tax treaty).

As explained at length in the Tempel Report[8] and by Chown[9] the other two systems, even with harmonization, do not achieve the degree of non-discrimination of the Separate system.

The Two-Rate system is not all that much inferior, however. Certainly, considerable difficulties arise with third countries not following this system, to the effect that the country with a Separate system will end up with a larger proportion of foreigner's investment income than if the Two-Rate system is in operation (in view of the big difference in the two systems that is likely between an equal overall rate on profits and the lower rate on distributions). Again, if the investment is not merely a portfolio one, but involves a branch or subsidiary of a foreign firm, distribution policy can be operated in a way which takes advantage of a country's Two-Rate system.

[8] See note 3.
[9] See note 6.

Even where the tax law may be reciprocal between two countries, the corporate power over its foreign income through distributional policy may be unequal.

In principle, these non-discriminations can be taken care of by tax treaties. But presumably Tempel prefers a generalized system which avoids discrimination rather than such ad hoc arrangements.

The Credit system involves greater problems of discrimination than the Two-Rate. Much depends on whether the foreign investor is granted some certificate which can be used to claim a credit against his domestic income tax liability—the French 'avoir fiscal'. If not, there is a clear discrimination between home and foreign investors in the country with the Credit system. This was previously the case in France, but now the avoir fiscal is being extended to nationals of some other countries. There is also discrimination between investments at home and overseas by a domestic investor if he gains a credit for corporation tax paid at home but not abroad. And even if a credit is granted abroad, it needs to be valid at home: but who bears the tax remission, the foreign or home government?

In principle, reciprocity and non-discrimination can be arranged between pairs of states by appropriately-drawn tax treaties. But again, Tempel is looking for general non-discrimination rather than its avoidance by such ad hoc arrangements.

The key difference between the Separate system and the other two, so persuasive for van den Tempel, is that the former gives general and automatic non-discrimination between Member States with a harmonized corporation tax and an unharmonized personal income tax, consistent with the aims of the EEC in its harmonization programme for direct taxation. The other two systems require extra provisions, series of international agreements or tax treaties, to ensure the two kinds of non-discrimination.

The vital question is: why is non-discrimination between the Member States so critical? It arises from the idea of neutrality, state-by-state, firm-by-firm, product-by-product, which dominates the thinking about taxation in the Treaty of Rome and subsequent Directives concerning taxation. And again, neutrality stems from the concept of a single, unified economy with a unified capital market.

As the writer has pointed out elsewhere[10], this aim of neutrality is more ideological than economic. Indeed the modern unified state, such as the UK, often needs to introduce discrimination, e.g. regional variations in taxes, as an act of policy. Much flexibility is lost through clinging too closely to the norm of non-discrimination.

Of course, this can be agreed, but the argument made that the discrimination flowing from a particular corporation tax structure is not a policy-chosen discrimination. This is a valid point, although the Tempel argument for the Separate system is absolutely not based on the proposition that it is a first stage to policy-chosen differentials in the Community harmonized corporation tax.

The British Reform, 1973–74[11]

As we have seen, there are some a priori domestic economic arguments in favour of the Separate system, in that the alternatives increase regressivity and possibly lower investment financed through retained profits. There are some arguments for it in the international sphere, to do with non-discrimination.

The sum of domestic and international factors do add up to some bias in favour of the Separate system. However, it is still unlikely to become the harmonized Community corporation tax structure.

There are two reasons. The substantive one is that it does conflict with equity ideas about the double-taxation of dividend income—that taxation at the full corporate rate plus full income tax on the dividend is an unfairly heavy tax burden on the shareholder. The more trivial reason is that the maximum inconvenience of administrative changeover would be suffered by EEC countries if all had to conform to the norm of a Separate system.

---

[10] D. Dosser, 'Economic Analysis on Tax Harmonization', in *Fiscal Harmonization in Common Markets*, ed. C. Shoup, Columbia University Press, New York, 1967, and D. Dosser and S. S. Han, *Taxes in the EEC and Britain: The Problem of Harmonisation*, Royal Institute of International Affairs/PEP, January 1968.

[11] For a summary of the technical details of this, see *Economic Progress Report*, No. 27, May 1972, HM Treasury.

The 'equity' (or perhaps better, political) point referred to is outweighing the economic suppositions about the superiority of the Separate system in the current British reform.

This goes ahead, formally introduced as at April 1973, although not effective for one year, because corporation tax is levied a year in arrears. Thus the rate for the new corporation tax was not announced in the 1973 budget. Since this, and other technical details, are not as yet clear, nor how the tax will work out in practice, it is too early for an evaluation, except in the general terms above[12].

[12] For another sceptical view, see Oliver Stanley, 'Nuts and Bolts of New Corporation Tax', *Times Business Section*, 22 February 1973.

5

The United Kingdom and the European Budget

by John Dodsworth

Introduction

ONE of the many difficulties facing members of an economic union is to devise a viable and mutually acceptable system of cost sharing for those policies which are to be jointly financed. Should the members be unable or unwilling to reach agreement at this level they will in effect preclude the coordination of a wide range of national policies. On the other hand a long or medium-term solution may be regarded, at least in potentia, as an important step towards a positive integration of the economies concerned.

In this chapter we shall be discussing an agreement on central budgetary provision concluded by the six founder members of the European Communities at The Hague in December 1969 and ratified by a Council decision in April 1970. The form of this agreement has, as we shall see, important implications for the UK as a new member of an enlarged community. Before going on to consider the details of this agreement, however, it may be as well to make a few general remarks concerning the role of a central budget.

In the early discussion surrounding post-war attempts to unify Europe, writers were fond of making a distinction between 'liberal' and 'planning' approaches to integration[1]. Both approaches were present in the drafting of the Treaty of Rome. On the one side was the ethic of competition, the freeing of trade, reliance on the market mechanism; on the other side there was the establishment of central institutions and agencies,

[1] See, for instance, R. Aron, 'Problems of European Integration', *Lloyds Bank Review*, April 1953.

and the longer-term perspective of an economic union. The Treaty of Rome both adopted the 'liberalist' solution *and* set up the machinery for central planning. Subsequent events have shown us that, with one or two exceptions, the 'liberal' element has been dominant. The emphasis of policy has been on eliminating barriers to trade and reducing distortive influences on competition: tendencies towards coordination or introduction of centrally controlled policies have, except in the special case of agriculture, been almost wholly resisted. The achievements of the EEC have thus been mainly on the 'negative' side of integration—that is, in the removal of discrimination[2].

It has been argued by the European Commission that this is essentially the first stage of integration. The progress in the future will depend on both, (i) consolidating the advantages of the customs union—by harmonizing taxation and other policies, and (ii) coordinating or centralizing certain functions now carried out by the member governments. It can be seen from this that a tension between 'liberal' and 'dirigiste' views of integration still remains. There is still pressure for the Community to exert a planning influence on certain national policies and for the member countries to accept a 'joint responsibility' in meeting certain common problems.

Those who advocate a 'positive' role for Community policies have a number of obstacles to overcome. Possibly the most difficult lies in convincing the national governments to transfer powers to supra-national agencies. In addition to this, however, there is still the problem in a large number of cases of actually financing centralized policies. The very nature of such policies (where benefits may often be spread in an indeterminate manner throughout the Community) makes it difficult to reach a satisfactory criterion for the sharing of costs. It was this difficulty with respect to the financing of the common agricultural policy which finally led to the agreement on joint financing concluded at The Hague. The agreement has an

---

[2] The term is used in this way by John Pinder. He defines its counterpart 'positive' integration as 'the formation and application of co-ordinated and common policies on a sufficient scale to ensure major economic and welfare objectives are fulfilled'. *Economic Integration in Europe*, ed. G. R. Denton, p. 145.

importance, however, not only because it reached a solution in apportioning the costs of the agricultural policy, but also because it represents a system of central budgetary provision which could potentially incorporate the type of positive policy advocated by those who wish to modify the dominant liberal conception of integration.

In the past few years, roughly between the Hague meeting and the Paris Summit of October 1972, a number of proposals for future positive policies have been made. The essential feature of these policies with regard to the budget is that they specify a desirable re-allocation of resources towards a particular region or a particular class. The central budget is advocated inter alia to give aid to certain industries, to help promote development in backward regions, and to give assistance to underprivileged groups. The difficulty here is that the expenditure pattern generated by any one of these policies is likely to favour some members of the Community rather than others. In the first place this may well be used to argue against the acceptance of a policy except as part of a political compromise. Secondly, unless some balance is achieved between different policies, or the method of cost-sharing is based on a benefit approach, the budget will tend to redistribute resources between countries, implying a balance of payments (and resource) loss for some members and a balance of payments (and resource) gain for the others.

This latter state of affairs is the position that the UK faces as a new member of the EEC. Both the means of raising revenue and the expenditure pattern of the budget will in the short run at least discriminate against the UK. This chapter essentially consists of a description of the ways in which this discrimination operates and an attempt to quantify the resulting balance of payments loss.

In the first of the three parts of the chapter we shall be reviewing the details of The Hague Agreement and details of the negotiated transitional arrangements for the UK which were announced in the British Government's 1971 White Paper (Cmnd 4715). This transitional phase covers the period from 1973 to 1979. Following this, in the second part, we shall be looking beyond the span of the White Paper to 1980, when the UK will be contributing to the European Budget under the direct income system designed for the Community. Finally, in part III, we shall be previewing some possible extensions of Community policy and modifications of the present structure of the budget which may serve to lower the UK net contribution to the budget.

I. THE EXISTING STRUCTURE OF THE BUDGET AND UK TRANSITIONAL ARRANGEMENTS 1973–79

The Hague Agreement

The Hague Agreement reaffirmed the will of the Member States to progress 'from the transitional period to the final stage of the European Community'[3]. It recognized that an important condition for this progress would be a relatively definite arrangement for the financing of the Common Agricultural Policy (CAP). The apportionment of the cost of the CAP between Member States had, naturally enough, been difficult to negotiate, but in addition to this the European Commission had consistently advocated changes in the actual method of financing. During a protracted debate the Commission had argued that the Community required its 'own resources', by which it meant explicit sources of revenue independent of the scale contributions provided for in the Treaty of Rome[4]. This development towards specific community resources replacing financial contributions had been suggested in the Treaty (Article 201) and was eventually accepted in principle by the Member States.

It was decided that following a transitional period certain sections of government revenue should be assigned directly to the Community. Under this scheme a lower limit to each member's contribution would be given by the transfer of 90 per cent of the revenue collected from the Common External Tariff and from Import Levies imposed on agricultural imports. In addition to this the Commission was empowered to collect the receipts corresponding to at most 1 per cent of the base of a harmonized value-added tax. Within these limits the actual

[3] Final Communique of the Conference of Heads of State or Government on 1 and 2 December 1969.
[4] Treaty of Rome: Article 200.

contribution could then theoretically be decided to cover the total expenditure commitment. The regulations therefore ensured as far as possible that Community expenditure would be financed entirely from 'Community resources', whilst also placing provisional upper and lower bounds on each member's contribution.

UK Transitional Arrangements 1973–79

Although the original six members of the EEC will conform to the new provisions by 1975, the UK will adapt to the system gradually over the seven year transitional period described in the 1971 White Paper[5]. The essence of this plan is that over the first five years of membership the UK will contribute an increasing proportion of the total budgetary cost rising from 8.64 per cent in 1973 to 18.92 per cent in 1977. This final figure was thought to indicate that by 1977 the UK contribution would be broadly proportional to its share in the total gross national product of an enlarged Community[6]. For the first five years then the UK contribution will be directly related to the level of budgetary expenditure. If we accept the government estimate of a £1600 million budget in 1977, then the gross contribution at the end of five years will be of the order of £300 million.

From 1978 onwards the direct income system will apply, necessitating the transfer of customs duties, levies and a percentage of VAT revenue as described above. The contribution will then be related to the level of expenditure not in a proportional manner but through the percentage of VAT required to balance the budget. However, the British Government negotiated certain safeguards to ensure that during the first two years of the system, i.e. 1978 and 1979, the year-to-year change in the contribution would not be excessive. This secondary transitional phase was designed to allow for the fact that the sources of revenue envisaged as the 'ressources propres' of the Community are not based on any criteria of proportionality or 'ability-to-pay'. Although the value-added tax may by 1978 be levied on a uniform basis of assessment throughout the Com-

[5] The United Kingdom and the European Communities, Cmnd 4715, paras. 91–96, HMSO, 1971.

[6] Ibid., para. 93.

munity[7], the transfer of receipts from the Common External Tariff and Import Levies will largely discriminate against those members who are relatively dependent on imports from non-Community sources. In this form the regulations are particularly unfavourable for the UK. Under present trading patterns the UK accounts for some 35 per cent of EEC agricultural imports from non-member sources and about 30 per cent of the corresponding imports of manufactured goods[8]. Comparing these figures with a UK share in GNP terms of 18 per cent is sufficient to show the possibility of a 'step' increase between the proportional basis of the 1977 contribution and the direct income basis of the 1980 contribution.

It is not possible, however, to take these figures as they stand. There will be certain compensatory pressures which will tend to lessen the UK's relative dependence on non-member imports. In the first place the introduction of an import levy system and EEC farm price levels will reduce substantially food import requirements and also transfer preferential treatment to Community suppliers. Secondly, the tariff protection accorded to EEC suppliers over the range of industrial products should enable them to expand their share of the UK market. In the second part of this paper we shall examine what effects these may have on the UK contribution in 1980. Before this, however, we can consider the disposal of the resources made available to the Community.

The Existing Structure of the Budget

To this point we have considered only the revenue side of the budget, that is, a member's gross contribution. We have seen that the regulations adopted will tend to favour some countries and discriminate against others. This disproportionality, introduced on the revenue side, is compounded when we consider the inter-country distribution of expenditure. A cursory glance at the present structure of the budget (see table 1) will be sufficient to show the extent to which it is dominated

---

[7] As discussed later this implies a harmonization of the VAT base, though not necessarily of the tax rates.

[8] The analysis was completed before Norway's withdrawal, and thus, the figures are based on a community of ten countries, comprising the present Six, Ireland, Norway, Denmark and the United Kingdom. Not a great deal of difference is made to the overall percentages.

by the financing of the Common Agricultural Policy. Approximately 90 per cent of revenue collected is channelled to farmers through the agricultural fund, FEOGA (Fonds Europeene d'Orientation et de Garantie Agricole). Only a relatively small portion of this expenditure (some £120 million) goes toward the re-structuring and modernization of farming in the Community. The remainder is paid in the form of export subsidies and market intervention to maintain price levels. In practical terms this has two corollaries.

Table 1. Budget expenditure 1971

	(in £mn)
European Agricultural Fund	1,096
Community Administrative Costs	62
Repayment to Member States to cover costs of collecting levies and duties	56
Eurat Research and Investment	28
European Social Fund	23
Food Aid	8
Total	1,273

Source: Cmnd 4715, Annex A.

The first is that the overall level of budgetary expenditure is closely related to the surplus supply position of agricultural products in the Community. In this respect the experience of the Six is well known. Over recent years increases in the production of certain commodities have outstripped the growth in Community demand. As a result surpluses have developed and accordingly there have been substantial increases in payments made to farmers through FEOGA. This growth in expenditure has acted as a constraint on the development of jointly financed projects in other areas. The Member States, faced with increasing and uncertain costs of the CAP, have generally been unwilling to add further to their financial commitment. In the past two years, however, the expenditure of FEOGA has shown some signs of stabilizing. Although it is too early to say, it may be that even a partial resolvement of the problem of surpluses will allow a diversification of Community projects and thereby give a more balanced appearance to the expenditure side of the budget.

The second inference from the existing structure of the budget is that the benefits accruing to any particular country will largely depend on the level of production attained in those products which are in excess supply with the Community. It is this which makes the CAP potentially a divisive force, imposing as it does a balance of payments burden on those countries which are net importers. If we compare the present member countries there are significant variations in the levels of self-sufficiency attained. Only France and the Netherlands are overall net exporters of regulated agricultural products, and as such emerge as the net beneficiaries of the CAP. For the UK, with only a small percentage of the working population engaged in agriculture, returns from a budget dominated by the agricultural policy are likely to be low. In this situation the best that the UK can hope for is a reduction in agricultural surpluses and a diversification of the budget into areas where benefits would be more closely related to contributions. From the inequity of the present situation, then, political pressures may be generated not only towards the reform of agriculture within the Community but also, perhaps, towards the introduction of a common industrial policy or common social or regional policies. The prospects for these are considered in the third section of the chapter.

II. THE UK CONTRIBUTION TO THE BUDGET, 1980

Adoption of an Import Levy System

It will be apparent from what has been said above that, in the context of the UK's accession to the EEC, agriculture will have a significance extending beyond its direct contribution to GNP. With regard to the budget the adoption of the Common Agricultural Policy will affect;

(i) payments into the budget (through import levies);
(ii) receipts from the budget (through market intervention and export restitution);
(iii) the overall level of FEOGA expenditure, to the extent that access to the UK market may reduce Community surpluses.

The EEC agricultural system is based on common marketing policies for all major products throughout the Community.

Free trade is permitted between member countries, though a set of common price levels is determined centrally. For some, though not all, products, prices are guaranteed to farmers, and in the event of a surplus supply in the market these are secured by means of intervention buying on behalf of FEOGA (this accounts for approximately 35 per cent of guarantee expenditure) and the subsidizing of high cost exports for sale on the world market (accounting for over 50 per cent of guarantee expenditure). The remaining expenditure of the guarantee section is assigned to production subsidies which are designed to limit imports, mainly of vegetable oils and fats. Domestic policy is necessarily supplemented by a common policy for external trade with protection from outside (low cost) suppliers mainly by the operation of variable import levies and tariffs, but also by quantitative and qualitative restrictions depending on the nature of the product involved.

A Theoretical Framework

To describe conceptually the transfers implied by the adoption of an import levy system it will be useful to begin with a standard partial equilibrium trade model for one commodity, as shown in figure 1. Initially it is assumed that there is a comparability between the imported good and the domestically produced good (allowing a total demand curve DD'), but that the domestically produced good is cleared from the market first and that therefore the demand for imports is a residual demand. The domestic supply curve is given by SS′ and the foreign supply curve, assumed to be perfectly elastic, by P_0P_0'. This gives the free trade c.i.f. price of OP_0.

If we wish now to compare a deficiency payments system (producer price $=OP_1$, consumer price $=OP_0$) with an import levy system (producer/consumer price $=OP_2$) care must be taken with the interpretation of the demand/supply schedules. They are no longer 'ceteris paribus' curves. The CAP will alter the prices of competing goods as well as the relative prices of inputs for domestic production. Comparing over time there will be sundry changes in income, population, changes in technology, etc. SS' and DD' should therefore be regarded as market equilibrium curves without the usual welfare implications.

Figure 1.

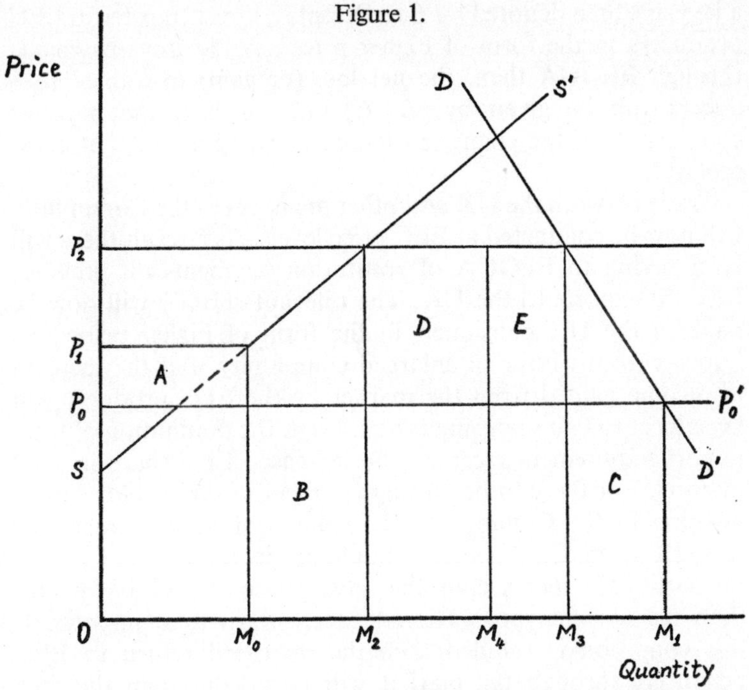

For the moment we shall assume that the foreign supply curve remains unchanged. The effect of imposing a threshold price (a minimum import price) OP_2, will be to increase domestic production by M_0M_2 and decrease consumption by M_1M_3; the new import requirement will thus be given by M_2M_3. Clearly this will affect both the level and distribution of returns to foreign suppliers. The reduction in the volume of imports valued at world prices (i.e. $B+C$) may be regarded as a gross loss of income to foreign producers. To derive the net loss (or gain) to foreign producers the remaining imports (M_2M_3) must be divided into two categories: those coming from EEC sources (M_3M_4) and those coming from non-EEC sources (M_2M_4). Levies are imposed only on the latter, which gives a total revenue collected equivalent to rectangle D. Ordinarily this would be retained by the central government but, as we have seen, under the direct income system 90 per cent of this revenue will be transferred to the central EEC budget. Imports from other members of the Community are not charged with a levy, the area denoted by E represents a direct transfer to EEC producers in the form of higher prices. Aside from payments through FEOGA then, the net loss (or gain) to foreign producers will be given by $(B+C)-E$, which is the negative counterpart of the change in the cost of imports of that commodity[9].

Trade between the UK and other members of the Community will now be conducted at EEC price levels. As a result there will be a saving to FEOGA of restitution payments on previous EEC (6) exports to the UK. The relevant subsidy will now be paid by the UK consumer, in the form of higher prices, on imports from within an enlarged community. But the increase in income gained from the market by the EEC producer will be subject to two opposing forces. First, the diminution of total import requirement; second, the increased EEC share in total imports. For there to be an improvement in the surplus supply position in the Community the volume of imports taken by the UK from EEC sources should be increased, that is, the proportionate increase in the EEC share should be greater than the absolute proportionate decrease in total imports. If this condition is fulfilled then the increased return to EEC producers through the market will be greater than the area indicated by E and correspondingly the loss of income incurred by non-EEC producers will be greater than $(B+C)$.

This situation involves certain areas of conflict. Consider the balance of payments effect of a marginal increase in UK agricultural output. It is necessary to take account not only of the opportunity cost of the resources utilized but also of the consequent abatement either in the UK contribution to the budget (D) or in the subsidy transfer to EEC farmers (E). To this extent those arguments which advocate import substitution through agricultural expansion are enhanced. But, a reduction in import requirement will have a deleterious effect on foreign producer income and, perhaps, on EEC producer income derived from the market. As explained above, the

[9] The overall increase or decrease in the cost of food imports will, of course, be an underestimate of the loss (or an overestimate of the gain) in foreign exchange attributable to the CAP. A partial approach takes no account, for instance, of the effects of all diverted expenditure, or of the opportunity cost of the additional resources required in terms of export or import substitution activity.

further that UK domestic supply is expanded (or demand contracted) the greater will be the increase in EEC share required to maintain the present volume of EEC imports. And, of course, the less that intra-community trade is developed the greater will be the budgetary cost of the CAP. For the UK an enlargement in the EEC share means initially a reduced revenue from import levies but a correspondingly larger direct subsidy to EEC producers. The major effect here is rather through the reduction in non-EEC producer income which, as Phillips and Ritson have pointed out[10], may well entail a reciprocal, and detrimental, effect on UK exports.

An Estimation of Import Levy Revenue

We turn to a quantitative appraisal of the situation and in particular to an estimation of the revenue derived from the imposition of import levies. As we have seen the main factors involved are: the degree of self-sufficiency attained by the agricultural sector in the home market; the level of protection adopted to divorce the Community market from world price levels; and the source composition of imports. The procedure followed in this section will be briefly to set out a central set of assumptions and the results derived from them. Certain of the assumptions will then be modified so as to show their relative importance and the sensitivity of the estimates.

The response of producers and consumers will be of central importance. We begin therefore in table 2 with the estimated demand and supply vectors for 1980 for each of the main leviable products. The new pattern of demand will result from substitution effects between certain foods; from substitution between food and non-food products; and from increasing levels of income. It was assumed that the demand for leviable products would be relatively inelastic to price changes: the average price elasticity of demand was −0.15. On the supply side the average expansion assumed over the products listed was 9.5 per cent; this compares with a figure of 8 per cent given by the 1971 White Paper[11].

[10] Truman Phillips and Christopher Ritson, 'Reciprocity in International Trade', *Journal of Agricultural Economics*, September 1969.

[11] Cmnd 4715, para. 87. The White Paper figure relates to 1977 and covers total agricultural output. As we shall see later the distribution of the increase between commodities is an important factor.

Table 2. Assumptions relating to UK agricultural trade—1980

Category	Demand 1969=100	Domestic Supply 1969=100	Assumed Price gap 1969=100	EEC share (%)
Wheat	87.5	107.9	100	40
Barley	93.6	115.8	100	—
Maize	91.2	—	100	—
Butter	76.2	131.9	70	50
Cheese	108.6	117.3	63	40
Sugar	96.1	105.4	50	10
Bacon/pork	103.8	104.8	43	100
Lamb	100.0	108.0	*	2
Beef/veal	100.0	109.3	*	60

The third column of table 2 pertains to the gulf between EEC prices and world prices. As a consequence of the system of voting on agricultural prices and the obvious need to arrest the growth in FEOGA expenditure it seems unlikely at the present time that EEC farm prices will show any increase in real terms during the next few years. Sicco Mansholt has indeed warned EEC suppliers that, following British membership, price increases should not be expected. World prices on the other hand are most definitely in a state of flux and for several products the gap between the EEC threshold price and the free trade price has narrowed significantly over the past two years. In the context of the debate on British membership this has been to the advantage of proponents of the Common Market for it diminishes those costs which are avoidable by staying out of the Community. The effect of an increase in the world price (relative to the EEC price) is to reduce the revenue collected under the heading of import levies and increase the income of non-EEC suppliers. If EEC prices are not put up then the increases in the price of dairy products and more recently in the price of sugar should help to allay some of the fears expressed on behalf of Commonwealth suppliers.

For the non-EEC producer there is a threatened loss of income not only in terms of a curtailment in import requirements but also through a diversion of trade toward EEC suppliers. The extent to which this diversion will take place cannot, at this stage, be stated with any great conviction. For some products (lamb, pigmeat) the issues are relatively clear;

for others (butter, sugar) the British Government has declared its intention of safeguarding the interests of traditional suppliers; for still others (grains) a quality factor limits the possible increase in the EEC share. Nevertheless a certain doubt must be attached to the assumed source composition and this will be remarked on later.

Table 3. Estimated revenue effects from adoption of the common agricultural policy

Category	(A)	(B)	(C)	(D)
Wheat	30.26	20.17	− 35.11	−16.70
Barley	− 17.32*	—	− 19.58	−62.04
Maize	26.53	14.28	− 15.99	7.56
Butter	50.51	50.51	− 21.35	50.89
Cheese	12.29	8.19	− 1.30	8.74
Sugar	9.18	1.02	− 7.20	1.61
Bacon/pork	—	11.26	− 20.48	28.08
Lamb	17.36	0.35	+ 5.07	5.83
Beef/veal	5.56	8.35	− 29.59	− 2.12
Total	151.69	114.13	−145.53	21.85

(A) Revenue from import levies and tariffs.
(B) Direct transfer to EEC producers in form of higher prices.
(C) Loss of income incurred by non-EEC producers.
(D) Change in the cost of selected food imports (net of protective duties).
* Export subsidy not included in total.

Results

Table 3 shows the revenue effects derived on the basis of the assumptions listed. For our discussion of the budgetary contribution the significant result is the revenue gained from levies and tariffs (column A). A breakdown by commodity shows that approximately 41 per cent of this revenue arises from imports of dairy products, 37 per cent from cereals and the remainder divided between sugar and meat. It is of interest to examine how the various changes contributed to this result. If, for instance, we had assumed that present consumption levels were to be maintained then the revenue from levies and tariffs would have been increased by some £30 million. But the changes involved on the demand side were not of equal weight. Almost all the saving can be attributed to the diversion of expenditure away from purchases of butter and the reduced demand for wheat. Similarly on the supply side the distribution of the increase in agricultural output is as significant as the global change. But, so far as the collection of duties is concerned, the supply response is not as critical as the variation in demand. If we suppose a zero supply response (as shown in table 4) then the consequent increase in the UK contribution to the budget would be less than £17 million. A 1 per cent increase in output over the relevant range implies a saving in this respect of a little over £1 million.

The division between payments into the budget and direct payments to EEC farmers in the form of higher prices (table 3, column B) is conditional upon the estimated share of EEC imports[12]. For instance there are no levies charged on imports

Table 4. Estimated revenue effects of simulated increases in domestic supply

(in £mn)

			Supply response		
Category		Nil	+5%	+10%	+20%
Wheat	(a)	32.61	31.14	29.67	26.73
	(b)	− 7.44	−13.27	−19.10	−30.76
Barley	(a)	4.87	− (1.78)	− (8.97)	−23.35)
	(b)	−13.31	−25.44	−42.39	−76.30
Maize	(a)	26.53	26.53	26.53	26.53
	(b)	7.56	7.56	7.56	7.56
Butter	(a)	53.80	53.28	52.77	51.73
	(b)	62.73	60.86	58.98	55.73
Cheese	(a)	14.96	13.33	11.70	8.44
	(b)	19.19	17.41	15.63	12.07
Sugar	(a)	9.71	9.46	9.21	8.71
	(b)	6.81	4.34	1.87	− 3.07
Bacon/pork	(a)	—	—	—	—
	(b)	44.59	27.59	10.60	−23.39
Lamb	(a)	18.31	17.71	17.11	15.91
	(b)	3.47	0.63	− 2.20	− 7.87
Beef/veal	(a)	7.90	6.56	5.22	2.54
	(b)	23.31	5.73	−11.85	−47.01
Totals	(a)	168.69	158.01	152.21	140.59
	(b)	146.91	85.41	19.10	−113.62

(a) Revenue from import levies and tariffs.

(b) Change in the cost of selected food imports (net of protective duties).

[12] Taken together these transfers represent a resource loss to the UK of perhaps £240–250 million.

of bacon/pork because of the assumption that an enlarged Community (including Ireland and Denmark) would be self-sufficient in that category. A supply increase here relates not to a saving in budgetary contribution but to a reduction in the direct subsidy. For butter imports this division is particularly important. By 1977, New Zealand producers will be guaranteed minimum sales in the UK of 136,000 tons of butter which accounts for something less than one half of the forecast import requirement[13]. Beyond 1977 there will be a continuation of the special arrangements for New Zealand but at some level to be agreed later. The effect of a further increase in the EEC share of, say, 10 per cent of total imports would reduce the revenue from levies (and increase the subsidy payment) by about £10 million. But it would in addition mean an increase in the loss of export earnings incurred by non-EEC suppliers of £13 million. For most commodities the increase in the EEC share proximates to that required to maintain the present volume of EEC imports: (it is in fact above the level required in the cases of sugar, bacon and maize but slightly below for wheat and cheese). This alone poses serious problems for traditional suppliers. But, as mentioned above, the situation in this respect has shown a certain improvement since 1969. Fortunately for non-EEC suppliers the full weight of the income loss has been attenuated by the narrowing of the gap between EEC and world prices. As shown in table 5 this has reduced the threatened loss of income to non-EEC producers by over £50 million.

Finally there is the question of the change in the net cost of imports. The 1971 White Paper states that 'the additional cost to our balance of payments on account of food imports seems unlikely to amount to more than . . . £50 million a year by the end of the transitional period'[14]. Other writers have since suggested that there may well be a reduction in the food import bill[15]. The estimate given here (table 3), column D) conforms to the opinion that the change will neither be substantially positive or negative. But a point made in the 1970

[13] Cmnd 4715, paras. 102–109.
[14] Cmnd 4715, para. 43.
[15] For instance the contributions by T. Josling and M. Miller to *The Economics of Europe*, ed. John Pinder, Charles Knight, 1972.

Table 5. Effects of changes in world prices relative to EEC price levels (£mn)

	1969 prices	+5%	+10%	+25%
Revenue from import levies and tariffs	186.20	175.31	164.43	131.77
Loss of income to non-EEC producers	198.07	181.21	164.36	113.77

White Paper should be reiterated. This particular figure is susceptible to large variations as a result of relatively minor changes in the assumed supply/demand response. The point is illustrated in table 4.

Revenue from the Common External Tariff

In this section we shall consider the effect of tariff changes on non-agricultural imports. The adoption of the EEC structure of tariff protection implies in effect a shift from one customs union to another with the ensuing transfiguration of both the volume and direction of British foreign trade. Fortunately to calculate revenue from the Common External Tariff it is necessary to concern ourselves only with changes in imports from non-EEC member countries and consequently the overall balance of trade effects are not examined. The analysis is further restricted to the static trade effects of tariff changes; that is, basically, changes in the formation of demand and the allocation of resources between export industries and import competing industries.

Under existing arrangements tariff barriers between the UK and other EFTA countries have been virtually eliminated whilst imports from Commonwealth countries enter either duty free or at preferential rates. Following entry into the EEC the dismantling of tariffs between the UK and the EEC will be accompanied by some degree of re-erection of tariffs between the UK and Commonwealth countries and, perhaps, the remaining EFTA countries. Associate membership has been offered to certain Commonwealth developing countries but more crucial from the point of view of estimating tariff revenue will be the result of negotiations between the non-candidate EFTA countries and present EEC members. A free trade agreement covering industrial products seems a probable outcome and in the following estimates an attempt has been made to indicate the likely effects of such an agreement.

Changes in the tariff structure as outlined above will affect both the overall level of imports and the source composition of imports. In the first place there will be a reallocation effect involving a substitution of imports for domestically produced goods or a replacement of imports by domestic production, depending on the direction of change in the effective rate of protection. A reduction in tariff rates will imply a displacement of domestic production and the consequent incurrence of adjustment costs. Secondly there will be a substitution of imports from EEC member countries for imports at present taken from non-member countries. This will consist of trade diversion—a transfer of income to less efficient but protected suppliers, and trade reversion—a transfer of income to more efficient suppliers disadvantaged because of the previous tariff position.

A simple static model[16] has been adapted to project changes in imports. It is assumed that:

(a) the overall level of imports is dependent on (i) the average price of imports (including the tariff) relative to the price of domestic substitutes, and (ii) the level of income;

(b) the demand for imports from any individual country depends on the relative landed price of imports from that country compared with the landed price of imports from other countries;

(c) there is an infinitely elastic supply curve for imports;

(d) there is full forward shifting of changes in tariff rates.

By the simplification of representing import price as a world price thus varying tariff rates it is possible to derive the proportionate change in the average landed price of imports in terms of tariff rates and market shares:

$$\dot{p} = \frac{t_1 s - t_0 n}{1 + t_0 n},$$

[16] Cf. H. G. Johnson, 'The International Competitive Position of the United States and the Balance of Payments Prospect for 1968', *Review of Economics and Statistics*, 1964.

where t_0 = present UK tariff charged on non-EFTA and non-Commonwealth imports,

t_1 = post Kennedy round tariff to be charged on non-member imports

n = share of non-EFTA or Commonwealth imports in total imports,

s = share of non-EFTA (10) imports in total imports[17].

The increase (or decrease in total imports of commodity i resulting from the adoption of the common external tariff is therefore:

$$E\, d_i\, \dot{p}_i\, M_i,$$

where $E\, d_i$ is the import price elasticity of demand for commodity i, and M_i is the total imports of commodity i.

It should be stressed that this approach does rest on the simplification of representing import price as a world price plus varying tariff rates. Strictly this applies only to a narrow range of homogeneous commodities and the approach therefore neglects the complexities of differentiated products and non-price competition. This proviso may prove nugatory as far as the level of imports is concerned. It is certainly an important factor in the consideration of market shares.

To calculate the source composition of imports it is necessary to calculate the relative price of member imports compared to non-member imports before and after the tariff changes. If we let a=the share of EEC (6) imports in total imports then the initial landed price of EEC (10) imports compared with the landed price of non-EEC (10) imports,

$$\mathrm{Pr}_1 = \frac{1 + \dfrac{n-a}{s}\, t_0}{1 + \dfrac{a}{1-s}\, t_0},$$

and the relative price following adoption of the common external tariff

$$\mathrm{Pr}_2 = 1 + t_1$$

[17] More generally this is the share of imports actually charged with the CXT (Common External Tariff).

which gives the final expression for imports from non-member countries following the tariff change,

$$[M_i\,(1+\dot{p}_i\,E\,d_i)]\;[s\,(1-\frac{\mathrm{Pr}_2-\mathrm{Pr}_1}{\mathrm{Pr}_1}\,Es_i)].$$

The first term reflects the change in the overall level of imports, the second the new source composition of imports.

Using the formulae given above an estimation was made of imports entering from non-member countries. Revenue from the common external tariff was calculated in two cases, (i) where there was free trade within the EEC bloc (10 countries), and (ii) where the free trade agreement was extended to the non-candidate EFTA countries. The following assumptions were made. Firstly imports were extrapolated to 1980 by means of an income elasticity of import demand calculated by a simple regression,

$$\log M = a + b \log \mathrm{GNP}.$$

A growth rate in GNP of 2.5 per cent per annum was assumed. Secondly the import price elasticities are estimates made originally by Ball and Marwah[18] and adapted for the UK by Balassa. They are as follows:

Finished manufactures	−2.68
Semi-finished manufactures	−1.42
Crude materials	−0.29.

Thirdly, a share elasticity of 0.66 has been used throughout.

Results

Table 6 shows the revenue from the common external tariff estimated for the two cases outlined above. The results tended to confirm the generally held opinion that the static gains from the customs union are small and are concentrated on manufactures of machinery, electrical plant, scientific instruments and plastics. Because of the small trade creation effect the estimates of tariff revenue were relatively insensitive to changes in the price elasticities. A more important factor was the diversion of imports from traditional sources. This trade diversion (and

[18] R. J. Ball and K. Marwah, 'The U.S. Demand for Imports 1948–58', *Review of Economics and Statistics*, 1962. B. Balassa, 'Trade Liberalization among Industrial Countries'. For further discussion of import price elasticities see chapter 2 in this volume.

reversion), however, was reduced substantially by the inclusion of non-candidate EFTA countries in the free trade area. On the assumption that a free trade agreement is offered to these countries, the revenue from the common external tariff on non-agricultural products was estimated to be in the region of £200 million. Along with the revenue derived from levies and tariffs on agricultural imports this will form the minimum UK contribution to the European budget.

Table 6. Revenue from the common external tariff (£'000)

Category	Present tariff revenue*	A %imports from non-member sources	A CXT revenue	B %imports from non-member sources	B CXT revenue
Chemical elements	5,865	54.3	4,754	43.5	3,822
Paints and dyes	1,467	52.3	1,884	26.2	972
Pharmaceuticals	512	48.4	631	30.4	402
Soaps & preparations	912	48.0	1,095	37.2	864
Fertilizers	1,357	35.7	367	33.3	343
Plastics	7,699	42.5	6,583	38.2	5,984
Other chemicals	2,673	62.9	3,999	56.4	3,628
Leather manufactures	851	80.7	2,150	76.9	2,052
Hides and furs	437	81.7	1,073	77.6	1,020
Rubber manufactures	2,562	72.1	4,146	65.5	3,783
Wood & manufactures	3,214	92.1	7,853	54.6	4,534
Paper manufactures	5,763	74.9	28,312	33.3	13,759
Textiles	11,880	57.2	22,489	40.2	16,264
Textile fibres	9,084	84.0	17,800	82.2	17,431
Non-metallic manufs.	4,619	37.5	3,762	26.0	2,691
Precious stones/metals	473	83.1	1,554	77.8	1,455
Iron & steel	6,974	52.1	8,066	31.2	4,916
Non-ferrous metals	2,291	85.0	5,394	80.5	5,111
Metal manufactures	3,211	50.8	3,992	35.0	2,818
Machinery (non-elec.)	48,689	49.7	39,372	39.2	31,551
Electrical plant	22,383	56.4	24,485	48.5	21,473
Transport equipment	17,638	60.9	19,828	56.0	18,351
Furniture	1,113	47.2	1,066	36.8	852
Clothing	5,724	58.3	15,202	48.4	13,591
Footwear	1,850	54.7	2,579	45.0	2,172
Scientific instruments	16,081	60.0	12,464	48.5	10,350
Misc. manufactures	6,482	64.8	7,157	52.2	5,827
Total	191,804		248,057		196,016

A. Exclusion of non-candidate EFTA countries.
B. Inclusion of non-candidate EFTA countries.

* 1969 figures. Some approximation was necessary in matching tariff breakdown and SITC categories.

The UK Gross Contribution

The gross contribution to the budget in 1980 will consist of 90 per cent of the revenue from the common external tariff and import levies plus a percentage of the base of a harmonized value-added tax. In the last two sections we have calculated that the minimum UK contribution will be of the order of £300–320 million (see table 7). In addition to this the financial arrangements allow for the collection of up to 1 per cent of the base of the VAT. The actual amount which Britain will contribute under this heading will be determined by the level of expenditure. As suggested earlier this will depend on the reduction of agricultural surpluses in the Community and the extent to which the member countries accept that there is a need for more 'positive' Community policies.

In the case that the full powers were invoked and a remittance of the full 1 per cent required, then the transfer of the VAT receipts could prove to be more significant than either the tariff revenue or import levies. Looking over a longer time period the VAT is the one source of revenue which is certain to

Table 7. The UK gross contribution to the budget

£ million (1969 prices)

Revenue from import levies	128.77
Revenue from tariffs	218.94
Less 10% collection costs	34.77
Minimum gross contribution	312.94
+ 1% value-added tax	235.00
Maximum gross contribution	547.94

keep pace with the growth of the economies of the Member States. Although manufactured imports will rise secularly, future initiatives to liberalize trade will tend to reduce revenue from tariffs. The revenue from import levies will decline in relative importance as the EEC becomes more self sufficient and as the gap between world and EEC prices narrows.

By the time the regulations are put into force the bases of value-added taxes in each of the countries must be harmonized, This does not present the difficulties that a rate harmonization would involve. Until a uniform rate system is adopted the members are free to zero-rate particular categories of expenditure. The major differences in the European value-added taxes do concern the level of rates rather than extent or coverage. The VAT is levied on most categories of consumer's expenditure. In the UK exemption is given for finance and insurance, land, betting and gaming, postal services, education and health. Extrapolating to 1980 suggests that the Commission, if exercising their full powers, could receive under the heading of VAT upwards of £235 million. This implies a possible maximum UK contribution to the budget of approximately £550 million (see table 7).

It would be hoped that unless the existing structure of the budget undergoes a major change over the next few years the maximum contribution to the budget would not be required. But this is again, of course, under the proviso that the costs of the CAP can successfully be contained. If payments to agriculture can be stabilized in real terms then the provision of 1 per cent of the VAT base will give scope to the future development of the European budget. If this is not the case then either the limit to the VAT must be extended or a fresh source of finance introduced to allow for a diversification of expenditure projects.

III. THE WIDENING ROLE OF THE EUROPEAN BUDGET.

There seems little doubt that for at least the next five or maybe ten years the bulk of the Community's 'own resources' will be used in subsidizing agricultural production in the member countries. It is fairly widely recognized, however, that there are potentialities in having a centralized budget with explicit sources of revenue. Recently, in particular during the period leading up to the Paris Summit of October 1972, a number of proposals have been made as to ways in which the budget may develop as an instrument of Community policy. In this section of the paper we will cover some of the more moderate of these proposals and briefly examine the implications of the Paris Communique. The introduction of new policies, and the provision of adequate resources for their implementation, will, as always, be dependent on the political climate. But it should be remembered that the UK will participate in the relevant decision-making processes and, as suggested earlier, the inequity of the present structure of the budget provides a strong argument for compensating changes. Most of the expenditure policies considered here certainly promise greater benefits for the UK than does the agricultural policy, but whether or not these benefits will be commensurate with the size of the UK contribution is a question left open at this stage.

Reform of the European Social Fund

It was recognized in the Treaty of Rome that the formation of a common market would, in its early stages, prove to be a disruptive force in the economies of the Member States. As workers moved from less efficient to more efficient occupations some transitional or structural unemployment would be inevitable. Initially the European Social Fund was set up to alleviate the effects on those left unemployed as a result of integration. In order to smooth the adjustment process the Fund was authorized to pay to the member governments one half of the costs of retraining and resettlement involved.

As can be seen from the summary of its operations provided in table 8, the range of activities covered by the European Social Fund has not been developed since it began operations in 1961. This, coupled with the fact that the resources placed at its disposal have been strictly limited, has meant that the ESF has made little impact on the member economies.

Although this has been disappointing the Council have recently accepted certain proposals which extend considerably

Table 8. Aid from the Social Fund in 1970 (u.a.)

	For retraining	For resettlement	Total
Germany	15,604,996	173,806	15,778,802
Belgium	1,426,930	—	1,426,930
France	3,925,727	236,693	4,162,421
Italy	14,283,477	238,741	14,522,218
Luxembourg	—	—	—
Netherlands	1,149,780	1,550	1,151,330
Community	36,390,900	650,791	37,041,701

Source: Fourth General Report on the Activities of the Community, 1970.

the powers of the Fund. The reformed European Social Fund is now empowered to act under two heads[19]:

(a) As a result of a Council decision, to intervene on every occasion that the employment position is, or is likely to be, threatened by specific measures of Community policy (industrial, commercial, agricultural, monetary) adopted by the Council or by jointly agreed action to facilitate the achievement of Community aims.

(b) To intervene in support of certain industries, firms or regions suffering from difficulties which are not a result of specific Council measures, but an indirect consequence of the functioning of the Common Market, or which hinder the smooth development of the Community. This intervention is intended to meet problems of long standing unemployment and under-employment of a structural nature, the training of highly skilled workers and the reintegration into the production process of handicapped or elderly workers, women and youth.

Clearly these passages may be interpreted in a wide or narrow sense. Theoretically the interventions of the Fund may now cover much wider areas of employment and regional policy. The extension of its activities will depend, however, on future policy decisions and the provision of resources. It has been decided that during the initial five year period at least half of the credits available will be devoted to activities in the second category.

A Common Industrial Policy

In the field of industrial policy there is also scope for the operation of a central budget. There seems to be agreement that some restructuring of industry may be desirable; that there is a need for joint action on scientific and technological matters; and that there may be possibilities in the joint financing of common infra-structure projects.

In its work in preparing the general principles for a Common Industrial Policy[20] the Commission has laid particular stress on

[19] *Bulletin of the European Communities*, September/October 1970.

[20] *Principles and General Datelines of an Industrial Policy for the Community*, Supplement to Bulletin 4—1970 of the European Communities.

the position of the advanced technology industries. In these industries the size of the firm is an important consideration. The contention is that, even in the presence of a customs union, firms in this field encounter difficulties in escaping from the limitations of a national market and hence are placed at a disadvantage with respect to outside competitors, in particular the large US corporations and their subsidiaries. The Commission claims that despite the fact that there has been a trend towards mergers—to exploit economies of scale and to face foreign competition—firms in the advanced technology industries still face national barriers. This fragmentation of the market is partly due to the dependence of such firms on public contracts (which are often the preserve of home industry) and on public funds provided by the national governments. The Commission concluded that there was a need:

(a) To eliminate in all sectors the obstacles hampering the formation of European transnational companies; and
(b) For this purpose to deploy in the advanced technology sectors the public funds available for industrial development[21].

On the first count it advised that the European Investment Bank should encourage the amalgamation of firms from different Member States by providing facilities for the financing of transitional mergers. On the second count it suggested that expenditure programmes which would 'establish competitive industrial structures' should become a major objective of the Community's industrial policy. This expenditure would take the form of Community Development Contracts which would be jointly financed by the Member States. The contracts would be awarded to firms in the advanced technology industries, but priority would be given to firms which had decided to engage in 'transnational co-operation'.

In addition to this plan to aid the technologically advanced sectors, the Commission has also proposed the establishment of two Community research organizations[22]. The European

---

[21] Ibid., p. 17.

[22] Commission Memorandum to the Council concerning Overall Community Action on Scientific and Technological Research and Development.

Research and Development Committee would be essentially a planning body which would submit to the Commission programmes for R & D co-operation within the Community. If these programmes were accepted by the Council they would then be implemented by a centrally financed European Research and Development Agency. The allocation of resources to this agency would be included in the Community budget and covered by the Community's 'own resources'. In its memorandum to the Council the Commission suggests a number of areas where joint action by the Member States could be productive. They include[23]:

(a) Organization of information and data centres;
(b) Steps to harmonize action to avoid duplication of effort;
(c) Organization of, or support for, training and respecialization courses for scientists, engineers and technicians;
(d) Granting financial aid for R & D programmes and specific industrial development projects conducted by public or private centres;
(e) Participation in the activities of other international scientific and technical organizations; and
(f) Direct implementation of R & D programmes which by their nature or their conditions of implementation would have to be carried out in a Community centre or at the initiative of or under the supervision of Community authorities.

A Community Regional Policy

Although there is clearly an overlap between a Community Regional Policy and the policies we have been discussing in the preceding paragraphs, the next stage in the development of the European budget is likely to be explicitly in terms of a policy for the regions. This was made clear in the communique which marked the end of the Paris Summit meeting. The new emphasis on, and support for, regional policy came from both the UK and from Italy, though for different reasons. Whilst Italy, and to some extent France, are concerned with the development of predominantly agricultural areas, the UK is primarily interested in the use of Community resources to help redevelop

[23] Ibid., p. 11.

declining industrial regions. A Common Regional Policy of the latter type would be of the greatest benefit to the UK and would thus tend to distribute budgetary expenditure in a more equitable fashion.

During the sixties the Community had adopted a typically negative stance on the issues of regional policy. The first responsibility of the Commission was to advise Member States on whether their regional aids were adjusted to be compatible with the strictures of Article 92 of the Rome Treaty[24]. This action was essentially 'negative' in so far as it was intended to minimize discrimination. More 'positive' action was taken through the existing institutions of the Community—the European Investment Bank, the European Social Fund and FEOGA, as well as by the European Coal and Steel Community—but this suffered both from a lack of coordination and from the inadequacy of the funds made available.

Within the original six members, pressure for regional policy came mainly from Italy which sought Community aid for the backward agricultural regions, like the Mezzogiorno. On this score the French attitude has long been that money devoted to regional development should be channelled through the European Investment Bank and take the form of an interest rate rebate rather than in direct expenditure policies. It was decided in September 1972, however, that £100 million should be provided over five years to stimulate development in agricultural areas of the Community.

At the Paris Summit in October 1972, mainly as a result of UK participation, the emphasis was changed from agriculture to an industrial regional policy. It was agreed at this meeting that 'a high priority should be given to the aim of correcting, in the Community, the structural and regional imbalances which might affect the realization of Economic and Monetary Union'. To this end the Member States gave an undertaking that their regional policies would be coordinated. But of greater significance was the agreement to set up a Regional Develop-

[24] This article states that 'any aid granted by a member state or by means of state resources in any matter whatsoever which distorts or threatens to distort competition by favouring certain enterprises or certain productions shall to the extent to which it adversely affects trade between the member states, be deemed incompatible with the Common Market'.

ment Fund before 31 December 1973, to be financed, 'from the beginning of the second phase of Economic and Monetary Union, with the Community's own resources'. This means that the UK gross contribution to the budget will be increased but one can confidently forecast that payments from a regional development fund will reduce the UK net contribution.

In a recent French survey[25] it was calculated that, if expenditure from a regional fund was to be aligned proportionately with present levels of national industrial aid, the share of the UK in a Community of nine would be in excess of 50 per cent—over twice the level of the UK contribution. The second largest beneficiary would be Italy (18 per cent) and payments to France would be around 5 per cent of the total.

Although this gives at best only a rough guide to the likely expenditure pattern it does show that an industrial regional policy could moderate some of the effects of the Common Agricultural Policy. The important question, as yet unanswered, relates to the overall size of the Fund and this will no doubt be the subject of bargaining within the Community for some years to come.

Conclusions

In the previous discussion we have been considering the first tentative steps in the creation of an autonomous central budget for the EEC. Neither the revenue nor the expenditure side of the budget should be thought of as formulated in a definitive manner. On the revenue side the system adopted for providing the Community with its 'own resources' will lead initially to an inequitable distribution of costs between the member countries. The system will tend to discriminate against those countries relatively dependent on imports from outside the Community. But the discrimination will be reduced as the revenue from tariffs and import levies declines in relative importance. For a number of reasons we can expect the revenue gained from the VAT to play an increasingly important part in the financing of Community policies. Whilst the revenue from the value-added tax will grow along with consumer's expenditure, revenue from levies and tariffs will be reduced by

[25] Prepared by M. Philippe de Castelbajac, Permanent Secretary of the French Government Regional Aid Agency.

increased self-sufficiency in agriculture, by a diminution of the gap between world and EEC food prices, and by future initiatives to liberalize world trade. Moreover, under the present system expansion of the budget will be based on increasing the percentage of VAT collected, thus ensuring that the marginal contribution to the budget is, in fact, reasonably proportional. Looking into the future the budgetary regulations may later incorporate other harmonized taxes, such as corporation tax or excise duties, or include an increased percentage of VAT. Within the limitation of the present provision, i.e. with a maximum of 1 per cent of the value-added tax base, a European budget of £2,200–£2,400 million (1969 prices) would be possible by 1980.

On the expenditure side the budget is at present confined almost exclusively to supporting the Common Agricultural Policy. The expenditure pattern is 'unbalanced' in the sense that the returns from the budget are centred on countries which have relatively large and relatively inefficient agricultural sectors. The 1971 White Paper forecasts that if the expenditure pattern of the budget remains unchanged, the UK returns from the budget in 1977 will amount to a little over 6 per cent of total expenditure, implying on the basis of a £1,600 million budget a net contribution in that year of £200 million. On the same assumption, and extrapolating to 1980 with the same growth rates, the UK net contribution to the budget (i.e. the net resource loss) is calculated to be in the range of £290 to £320 million. This would require a VAT contribution of between 0.4 per cent and 0.5 per cent of the base.

But forecasts of budgetary expenditure can only be extremely tentative at this stage. For one thing it is difficult to gauge the likely effect of current reforms in EEC agriculture. The latest figures suggest that the White Paper may have underestimated the rate of growth in agricultural expenditure. If this is the case then the net contribution given above will also be an underestimate.

Whatever success is achieved in moderating the costs of the CAP will, in addition to lowering the UK net contribution, also have a significant influence on the structure of future budgets. As we have seen there is no shortage of proposals advocating more positive roles for Community policies, and many of these would require an extension of budgetary operations. The new Regional Development Fund when it comes into existence will be financed from the Community's 'own resources', and its expenditure priorities should ensure a higher correlation between receipts and contributions. For the UK the balance of payments and resource loss to be sustained in the 1980s as a result of the working of the budget will depend critically on overall expenditure on regional policy and the introduction of other new policies.

Even so one would have difficulty in predicting whether or not the European budget will develop as an instrument of Community policy. In part it will depend on the success attained in implementing other aspects of economic and monetary union. The adoption of a common currency in particular will impose constraints on national economic policies creating a need not only for a central monetary policy but also in time for a truly Federal budget.

6

Tax Harmonization Policy from the Point of View of the Commission

by Klaus Schneider*

The Objectives of Tax Harmonization

THE Commission of the European Community has never considered tax harmonization as an aim that must be pursued for its own sake. Attempts at advocating the approximation of tax legislation as an end in itself are misguided. In fact, tax harmonization is an instrument that serves to promote the process of economic, social and political integration in the Community.

The following general guidelines were stated by Mr. Haferkamp, Vice-President of the Commission, when replying in the European Parliament to a question on the subject:

> We want to carry tax harmonization as far as is required by the objectives of the Common Market. We must harmonize where this is necessary to eliminate tax frontiers and avoid distortions of competition; we must harmonize in order to facilitate mergers across the internal frontiers of the Community and to help build up a European capital market. We must also harmonize as a part of the work to be done before we can arrive at a common economic policy, and quite simply with a view to achieving the aims of a number of common policies in various sectors of our activity.

At present three criteria for tax harmonization can be distinguished.

* The author wishes to make it clear that the opinions expressed in this paper are his own and not those of the Commission of the EEC.

(*i*) *Furtherance of the Common Market*

From this point of view it is the task of tax harmonization to ensure that the tax legislation to the Member States does not hinder the creation of an area in which the movement of persons, goods, and capital and the supply of services can develop freely without distortion of competition.

(*ii*) *Development of Economic and Monetary Union*

So far, the relationship of tax harmonization to economic and monetary policies has not had a high priority. Coordination of economic policy, in fact, although laid down in the Treaty of Rome as necessary if the goals of the Community are to be reached, has been a subject more of discussion than of action. This situation, however, is bound to change.

Now that we are actively aiming at economic and monetary union, taxes must more than ever be considered, from the point of view of economic management at the Community level.

In order to make it possible to use taxes as instruments of management at Community level, tax harmonization might be needed. In the context of a common stabilization, industrial and regional policy for example, taxes on company profits might be used as an instrument to influence private investment. Very often tax rules, those on tax incentives for example, are not sufficiently clear and precise for the Community institutions to be able to measure their presumed efficiency and their impact on private investment. For that reason, certain areas of taxation may have to be included in the process of harmonization, quite apart from the Common Market aspect.

The two criteria for tax harmonization are closely interrelated. Indeed the Resolution of 22 March 1971 on the achievement by stages of economic and monetary union *explicitly* places free movement of products and of factors of production, together with the postulate of undistorted competition, in the context of further integration in the fields of common economic and monetary policy. Many important measures for tax harmonization in the EEC, already proposed by the Commission, are still undecided at Council level. Most of these proposals could certainly be adopted without further progress in the field of common policies. Such progress, however, would make much easier the future stages of tax harmonization.

(iii) Provision of 'Own Resources' or European Budget Revenue
The European budget requires a certain measure of tax standardization, but for the time being this will in fact be limited to the VAT.

The budget of the Community was formerly financed mainly by contributions from the Member States. According to the Council Decision of 21 April 1970, full replacement of the financial contributions by the Community's own resources is to be reached in stages by 1 January 1975. In an intermediate phase (1 January 1971–31 December 1974) the Community budget will be financed partly from its own resources (customs duties, agricultural levies and other charges), and partly from financial contributions. In the final stage, beginning 1 January 1975, the Community budget will be financed completely from its own resources.

In the final stage, a new source of revenue will be added to the resources already assigned to the Commission in the intermediate stage. In accordance with Article 4 of the Decision, this revenue will consist of VAT receipts 'resulting from the application of a rate which must be at most 1 per cent of the tax base to be laid down uniformly for the Member States according to Community rules.'

The introduction of this uniform basis of assessment means that virtually all elements of VAT, which have so far been left to the autonomous decision of Member States, must be harmonized, with the sole exception of rates.

Tax Harmonization Processes in the European Community
Before reviewing existing and prospective implementation of the harmonization of taxes for the achievement of the three kinds of objective, it will be useful to note the *process* by which harmonization is achieved.

Pursuant to Articles 99 and 100 of the Treaty of Rome it is the task of the European Commission to put forward to the Council of Ministers proposals for harmonization of tax legislation. Although the Commission itself has the power to submit to the Council on its own initiative any proposal it thinks necessary in the fiscal field, it thought it advisable to involve representatives of the national governments in the preparatory work. Council decisions in the field of tax harmonization are normally reached by the following procedure:

1. Preliminary studies result in the drafting of a working document by the Directorate-General responsible for tax harmonization;
2. this working document is discussed by a working party composed of tax experts from the Ministries of Finance, under the chairmanship of a senior official of the responsible Directorate-General;
3. thereupon a draft directive is worked out and discussed by a standing committee of the heads of revenue departments of the Member States under the chairmanship of a representative of the Commission;
4. the draft directive is adopted by the Commission on the proposal of the member responsible. After adoption by the Commission, the proposal is submitted to the Council;
5. then there is the mandatory consultation by the Council of the European Parliament and the Community's Economic and Social Committee;
6. thereupon, the Commission's proposal and the opinions rendered by the above-mentioned consultative bodies are examined by a specialized committee of the Council;
7. the proposal and opinions are then examined by the Committee of Permanent Representatives of the Member States;
8. After all these preparatory procedures, the discussion in the Council takes place. Decisions on proposals of the Commission in the field of harmonization of legislation can only be taken by the Council acting by means of a unanimous vote. These decisions usually take the form of Directives to the Member States. Under Article 189, a Directive is binding on Member States as to the results to be achieved, but governments are free to select the form and means of incorporating it into their national legislation.

General Taxes on Consumption

When on 11 April 1967 the Council adopted the first two Directives on value-added tax[1], the road was cleared for achieving the first aim in the harmonization of turnover taxes, which was to abolish the cumulative multi-stage taxes and replace them by

[1] EEC *Journal officiel*, 71, 14 April 1967.

a non-cumulative system. By 1 January 1973 VAT had—after some delays[2]—been introduced in all Member States of the Community of the Six.

The progress made, however, represents a first step only. Although application of the rules contained in the first two Directives helps to ensure that, as far as competition is concerned, the tax is neutral in its impact on trade across the frontiers, it is not sufficient to ensure unification of the basis of assessment, nor will it be possible in this way to eliminate the taxes on imports, the rebates on exports or the checks that are called for by these measures.

Under Article 4 of the first Directive of 11 April 1967, the Commission is to submit to the Council proposals as to how and within what period the harmonization of turnover taxes can achieve the aim of abolishing the imposition of tax on imports and the rebates on exports in trade between Member States, while ensuring the neutrality of those taxes as regards the origin of the goods or services. In this connection, particular account must be taken of the relationship between direct and indirect taxes, which differs in the various Member States, of the effects of an alternation in tax systems on the tax and budget policy of Member States and of the influence which tax systems have on conditions of competition and on social conditions in the Community.

Article 19 of the second Directive further provides that in the interest of the Common Market the Council is in the proper time to adopt, on a proposal from the Commission, the appropriate Directives to complete the common system of value-added tax, and in particular to restrict progressively or to abolish measures adopted by Member States in derogation from this system, so that national systems of value-added tax may be brought into alignment, thereby preparing the way for the attainment of the objective set out in Article 4 of the first Directive.

Pursuant to the Council decision of 21 April 1970 on replacing the Member States' financial contributions by the Community's own resources[3], a major step forward towards *further* harmoni-

[2] EEC *Journal officiel* L 320, 20 December 1969; L 283, 24 December 1971; L 162, 18 July 1972.
[3] EEC *Journal officiel* L 94, 28 April 1970.

zation of the VAT systems in the various member countries will have to be taken at an early date.

In accordance with Article 4 of this decision, part of the Communities' own resources will be obtained by applying a rate, not to exceed 1 per cent, to a basis of assessment fixed *uniformly* for the Member States according to Community rules. The unification of the basis of assessment of VAT consists in fixing a common field of application of the tax, especially in respect of:

(a) taxable persons;
(b) taxable and tax-exempt types of turnover;
(c) special systems;
(d) procedures for determining the bases of assessment.

Community rules on this subject fit, then, tidily into the measures that have to be taken if the final goal of the VAT harmonization—abolition of internal tax frontiers—is to be achieved.

The resolution of the Council and of the representatives of the Governments of the Member States of 22 March 1971[4] on the achievement by stages of economic and monetary union confirms the principle whereby, at the end of the process leading to this union, the Community is to 'constitute an area within which persons, goods, services and capital will move freely and without distortion of competition'. Among the concrete moves to be made during the first three-year stage that began on 1 January 1971, the Council in connection with VAT referred to its decision of 21 April 1970 on the Community's own resources.

During the first stage of the proposed economic and monetary union, i.e. by 31 December 1973 at the latest, the Council must decide on the relevant proposals from the Commission and agree on a uniform basis for assessing VAT. The Commission has already prepared a first draft of such proposals. It takes account of the following two aspects:

(a) the need of a uniform basis for assessing VAT in view of the collection throughout the Community of that part of VAT which accrues to the Communities as own resources;

[4] EEC *Journal officiel* C 28/1, 27 March 1971.

(b) the need to harmonize the common VAT system with a view to ensuring neutrality in respect of competition and to abolish border tax adjustments among Member States.

Measures to be carried out after 1 January 1974

The measures to be taken in the field of value-added tax after 1 January 1974, must be carried out in parallel with and at the same time as the establishment of economic and monetary union. They relate mainly to the alignment of the national VAT rates and action to eliminate the taxation of imports and rebates on exports in intra-Community trade.

Harmonization of the level of national VAT rates should be carried out in stages; this would enable the necessary changes in national legislation to be made gradually, avoiding sharp upheavals or unduly frequent alterations.

Pattern of VAT rates in January 1973

	Reduced rate	*Intermediate rate*	*Standard rate*	*Increased rate*
United Kingdom (to be introduced 1 April 1973)			10	
France	7	17.6	20	33.33
Belgium	6	14	18	25
Netherlands	4	—	16	—
Italy	6	—	12	18
temporarily:	1 and 3			
Germany	5.5	—	11	—
Luxembourg	5	—	10	—
in certain cases:	2			
Denmark	—	—	15	—
Ireland	5.26	11.11	16.37	30.26

In some countries (e.g. Netherlands, Ireland, Denmark) zero-rates the exception, whereas in the UK zero-rating is planned in a very large scale.

The first stage of alignment of the rates could be implemented by:

(a) applying a very small number of tax rates, in principle only two, namely a standard rate and a reduced rate;

(b) drawing up common lists of goods and services, broken down by the tax rates applying to them;

(c) fixing the upper and lower limits of bands within which the Member States may themselves fix the level of their tax rates.

Priority should be given to reducing to two the number of rates applying in each Member State, so as to simplify VAT collection procedures both for taxpayers and the tax administration.

Collection of the tax would, of course, be greatly simplified by applying a single rate of value-added tax; in view of the conditions in the Member States, however, it would be difficult to propose one single rate. The plan therefore could be to apply a reduced rate to consumer goods and certain services while the remaining goods and services are to be subject to the standard rate. The problems of choice of the number of rates, especially zero-rates, will undoubtedly lead to prolonged discussions in the new situation of the enlarged Community.

The alignment of national rates will, of course, be meaningful only if these rates are applied to the respective common lists of goods and services.

The individual Member States, guided by their particular requirements, could, in the first stage of approximation, fix these rates within fairly wide bands whose upper and lower limits would be determined by the Community. For the standard rate, the working hypothesis under discussion provides for a band of 12 per cent to 18 per cent or 13 per cent to 19 per cent; for the reduced rate, the limits could reasonably be 5.5 per cent and 7.5 per cent. This would give the Member States some room for manoeuvre. It should be emphasized, however, that these rates are no more than working hypothesis which may perfectly well be changed as soon as more information is available on the likely budgetary, economic and social consequences of such an alignment. Econometric studies of this type, based on common hypotheses, are currently being made at national level.

For the rest, the resolution of 22 March 1971 on the achievement by stages of economic and monetary union provides that before the end of the first stage, in other words by 31 December 1973, the Council is to examine those studies and proposals which the Commission will have made on the alignment of the VAT rates.

The following stage or stages of the alignment of rates would have to be timed to coincide with the abolition of taxes on imports and refunds on exports, together with all checks and related formalities. The gaps between the upper and lower limits of the bands of the two VAT rates would therefore have to be reduced sufficiently to rule out the danger of serious distortions of competition or an unduly large risk of tax evasion.

Once the tax rates have been sufficiently aligned, and harmonization of the common value-added tax system has been completed, it will be possible in intra-Community trade to abolish the checks and VAT formalities at the internal frontiers which are an impediment to the free movement of goods and services.

Application of VAT in intra-Community trade could then be based on the principle that the combined territories of the Member States form one single area for the purposes of VAT. Transactions involving the supply of goods between Member States and the supply of services within the Community would then be treated as business done within one country; the part supplying the goods or the service, who is subject to value-added tax in one Member State, will invoice the amount of tax owed in that Member State, while the purchaser of the goods or beneficiary of the service who has to pay tax in another Member State may deduct the amount from his tax liability.

The system of taxation of imports and refunds on exports will consequently cease to be applied in intra-Community trade but continue to be applied in trade with non-member countries.

Application of the system, involving the deduction within the Community of value-added tax across the internal frontiers, naturally raises the problem of compliance with the principle of allocation of VAT receipts to the state of destination. One could envisage a system of clearing between the Member States with a view to computing the amount of VAT collected in the country of origin and allocating it as accurately as possible to the country of destination.

The moves which the Commission has to make in the field of VAT harmonization can be summed up as follows:

(a) Submission of Commission proposals to the Council on how the basis of assessment of value-added tax can be unified until early 1973;

(b) submission of a Commission proposal to the Council on the fixing of bands for the first stage of the alignment of VAT rates before the end of 1973.

Excise Duties

Excise duties should be harmonized for much the same reasons as turnover taxes. Here, too, the aim is to ensure the free movement of goods in the Community while avoiding distortions of competition. This is expressly confirmed in the resolution of 22 March 1971 on the achievement by stages of economic and monetary union. As regards the time schedule, the resolution specifies that within the first three-year period the Council, on a proposal from the Commission, is to decide on measures concerning harmonization of the structures of excise duties, that is 'harmonization of the scope and base and of procedures for levying excise duties, in particular those having an appreciable effect on trade'.

The first need is to determine which excise duties are to be retained and harmonized at Community level. In the opinion of the Commission the list should comprise five types of excise duty, viz. (a) mineral oils; (b) tobacco; (c) spirits; (d) beer; and (e) wine. The importance of these types of excise duty for revenues is well known, and the following criteria were applied in choosing them:

(i) a comparatively high yield is required;
(ii) the basic necessities of life should not be taxed;
(iii) goods used in industry as raw materials, productive equipment or auxiliary materials should not be taxed;
(iv) consideration must be given to social policy;
(v) consideration must be given to health policy;
(vi) there may be implications in relation to the developing countries;
(vii) there is a possibility of product substitution (competition).

One can start from the assumption that the excise duties on mineral oil and manufactured tobacco will in any event have to be maintained and harmonized. They are levied in all Member States and yield such high receipts that it would hardly be possible to offset by an increase in other taxes the shortfall that would occur if these duties were abolished.

Considerations of public health are a major argument in support of the maintenance and harmonization of the excise duty on spirits, a duty levied in all Member States.

None of the criteria referred to appears to militate in favour of the excise duties on beer and wine. In respect of the excise duty on beer it can at least be argued that all Member States are levying it and that in most of them its yield, while not significant, is not negligible. This is a border-line case that is being judged on a fairly pragmatic basis.

To support the maintenance of the excise duty on wine, whose yield is in fact low and which is not levied in Italy and only on sparkling wines in Germany, reference is made to the high degree of substitutability between beer and wine. If excise duty is levied on beer, so the argument runs, there should also be an excise duty on wine, although Italy and Germany have strong reservations about it, especially concerning the difficulties of collection. It Italy, for instance, about 1.5 million wine growers would have to be subjected to controls. Other Member States and the Commission, on the other hand, do not share these reservations, pointing out that the introduction, under the Common Agricultural Policy, of the common organization of the market in wine already calls for the institution of a system of control at producer level: no additional controls would therefore be necessary. The levying of the excise duty on wine would, on the other hand, facilitate implementation of the Common Agricultural Policy in this field.

So much, then, for the five types of excise duties that should be maintained and harmonized.

No consideration has been given to a Community excise duty on coffee, tea and sugar, although in some Member States the receipts are of a certain significance. Indeed, these duties *should be abolished*. The *excise* duty on coffee and tea runs counter to the objectives of the policy on development aid, while the excise duty on sugar falls on a product that is partly a basic food and partly a raw material for industry.

Like the excise duties on coffee, tea and sugar, all other excise duties involving border tax measures in trade between Member States would have to be abolished once the tax frontiers have been fully dismantled. But those excise duties which, in trade between Member States, give rise neither to an imposition of tax on imports coupled with refunds on exports nor to checks at the frontier, could be maintained beyond that point in time.

In all Member States, with the possible exception of Italy, the loss of revenue would be very small if all these excise duties were abolished and only the five major excise duties maintained.

As in the case of the value-added tax, one will have to begin by harmonizing the structures of the five types of excise duty that would be maintained. The aim is to harmonize all sections of the structures which have a direct or indirect impact on the conditions of competition, particularly the scope of the duty, the basis of assessment, the type of duty (specific or ad valorem), the exemptions, the point at which the duty becomes payable, the rules to be applied to imported or exported products, the methods of collection and the way the duty is paid. In certain cases it will also be necessary to harmonize other elements such as the checks, the rules governing deferment of excise duties, etc.

As with the harmonization of value-added tax, there will have to be an alignment of the tax rates if border tax measures and border checks are to be abolished. There are no concrete ideas yet on the level of these common rates or rate brackets.

In accordance with the resolution of 22 March 1971 on economic and monetary union, quantitative studies of the budgetary, economic and social implications of an alignment of these rates will have to be undertaken, studies which will have to be submitted to the Council before the end of the first three-year stage.

In its drive to harmonize excise duties in the first stage of the establishment of economic and monetary union, the Commission has therefore concentrated on two points:

(a) submission of an outline directive listing in particular the five types of excise duty to be maintained and harmonized;
(b) submission of directives on harmonizing the structure of each of these excise duties.

Propositions embodying these lines of thought were submitted by the Commission to the Council on 7 March 1972[5].

[5] EEC *Journal officiel* C 43, 29 April 1972.

They consisted of draft Directives on the programme of excise tax harmonization and on the subject of harmonization of the structure of wine, spirits and beer excises. Also the establishment of an Excises Committee was proposed. In the general draft Directive, the five harmonizable excises listed earlier must all exist in Member States from 1 January 1974. Harmonization of their structures is dealt with in separate directives. In addition, excises other than the principal five must be phased out from the moment that fiscal frontiers are abolished. The Member States, however, shall retain the ability to maintain or even to introduce new duties and taxes provided they do not involve, in trade between Member States, border tax adjustments.

On the basis of an amended proposal of 20 November 1970 for a Directive on the structure of the excise duties on manufactured tobacco[6] the Council adopted that Directive on 19 December 1972. In the field of duties on mineral oils, on 28 December 1970, the Commission submitted to the Council a proposal on the harmonization of excise duties on liquid hydrocarbons for use as combustible fuels[7]. There will be other proposals in this field.

Exemption from Import Duties in International Passenger Traffic

Even with customs union completed, inter-Community trade is not yet free from border tax measures and the related checks. Removal of these tax frontiers will still take a fair number of years (see harmonization of value-added tax and excise duties). For the private individual travelling within the Community this situation is obviously unsatisfactory, and the European citizen has good reason to be puzzled when told that there are no longer any customs frontiers while he has to put up with other frontiers of a similar nature, the tax frontiers.

To ease this situation the Council, on a Proposal from the Commission on 28 May 1969, adopted a Directive on the harmonization of laws and regulations relating to exemption from turnover taxes and excise duties on imports in international passenger traffic[8]. The principal elements of this directive, which entered into force on 1 January 1970, were:

---

[6] EEC *Journal officiel* C 4, 18 January 1971.
[7] EEC *Journal officiel* C 14, 11 February 1971.
[8] EEC *Journal officiel* L 133, 4 June 1969.

(a) tax emption for goods imported from one Member State into another up to a total value of 75 units of account per person, provided the goods are carried in the traveller's personal luggage and are not commercial in character;
(b) tax exemption for specified quantities of manufactured tobacco (for instance 200 cigarettes), alcoholic beverages (for instance 1 bottle of whisky), wine (2 litres), perfumes, coffee and tea.

On 22 July 1971, the Commission submitted to the Council a Proposal for a second Directive on the harmonization of laws and regulations relating to tax exemption in international passenger traffic[9]. The aim was twofold:

(a) The first Directive of 28 May 1969 must be adapted to one of the aims of the Resolution of 22 March 1971 on the establishment by stages of economic and monetary union. This Resolution in fact calls for 'the progressive extension of tax exemptions granted to private persons on crossing intra-Community frontiers' in the first three-year stage. The Proposal therefore includes a further extension of these exemptions.
(b) There also has been a need to remove certain difficulties encountered in implementing individual provisions of the Directive of 28 May 1969.

Practical proposals:

(a) Doubling the tax exemption from 75 units of account to 150 units of account.
(b) Doubling the quantities of cigarettes, coffee and wine that may be imported free of tax.
(c) Removing the quantitative limits on tax-free imports of tea and perfume.
(d) Making minimum exemptions for persons resident on a frontier and for frontier workers (so far the granting of exemptions has been optional).
(e) Abolishing the duty to declare goods under the arrangements for tax-free entry. (There is, indeed, little point in granting travellers tax exemptions, yet requiring them to put up with checks and to declare goods in order to benefit from these exemptions.)

---

[9] EEC Commission document (71) 706 final, 22 July 1971.

The concept 'traveller' in the first Directive gave rise to special difficulties, as some Member States (Belgium, France, Luxembourg) were putting a very narrow interpretation on it. Under this practice, certain exemptions were made subject to the condition that to benefit from them, a person must have stayed more than 24 hours in the country involved. The Commission disagreed with that restrictive interpretation and urged that the concept be interpreted broadly, in line with the meaning and purpose of the Directive. The Commission takes the view that the Member States mentioned were infringing the Directive and therefore initiated the procedure under Article 169 of the Rome Treaty. Subsequently, the Member States concerned annulled their 24-hour condition.

Finally, it should be mentioned that under the first Directive the value of goods which may be imported tax-free in passenger traffic between a non-member country and the Community was fixed at 25 units of account while tax exemption for specified goods (cigarettes, spirits, etc.) continued to be governed by the various national rules. Under the Commission proposal for the second Directive, no change has been foreseen in these provisions. This second Directive, slightly modified in relation to the Commission Proposal (exemption of only 125 units of account, 300 cigarettes instead of 400, etc.), has been adopted by the Council on 12 June 1972[10]. In the meantime, two more Proposals in this field have been submitted to the Council, concerning tax-free shops and imports of small packages[11].

Indirect Taxes on the Raising of Capital

At an early stage the Commission looked into the effects of indirect taxes on the raising of capital, that is the duty chargeable on contribution of capital to companies and firms, and the stamp duty on securities. It found that both taxes give rise to discrimination, double taxation and disparities which interfere with the free movement of capital in the Community.

In the Council Directive of 17 July 1969 concerning indirect taxes on the raising of capital[12], it was decided to harmonize the duties chargeable on contribution of capital to companies and

---

[10] EEC *Journal officiel*, L 139, 17 June 1972.
[11] EEC *Journal officiel*, C 113, 28 October 1972.
[12] EEC *Journal officiel* L 249, 3 October 1969.

firms (capital duty) and to abolish the stamp duty on securities.

From 1 January 1972, the harmonized capital duty is charged on the transactions listed in Article 4 of the Directive, including:

(a) the formation of a limited company;
(b) the conversion into a limited company of a company, firm or legal person which is not a limited company;
(c) an increase in the capital of a limited company by contribution of assets of any kind.

Certain other transactions may be subject to the harmonized duty, for instance an increase in the capital of a limited company by capitalization of profits or of permanent or temporary reserves, as well as a loan taken up by a limited company.

Article 5 defines the basis of the assessment of the duty on these transactions. Articles 6, 8 and 9 list a number of exemptions and special systems.

Article 7 deals with the harmonization of the rate, specifying that the rate of capital duty may not exceed 2 per cent or be less than 1 per cent. In certain cases (e.g. mergers), this rate is reduced by a half. In the same Article, the Commission is called upon to propose a common rate for capital duty. Meanwhile, the Commission on 1 February 1971 submitted to the Council the proposal for a Directive on the fixing of common rates for capital duty[13]. The Commission proposes a common rate of 1 per cent and a reduced rate of 0.5 per cent.

Article 11 lays down details on the abolition of the stamp duty on securities, also scheduled to become effective on 1 January 1972.

The Proposals on rate harmonization, which will apply from 1 January 1976, were adopted by the Council on 6 December 1971, subject to consultation with the new Member States[14].

Direct Taxes

On 26 June 1967, the Commission submitted to the Council a 'Programme for the Harmonization of Direct Taxes'[15]. A second Commission Memorandum of 5 March 1969, also laid

[13] EEC *Journal officiel* C 34, 14 April 1971.

[14] In this context the Commission submitted a proposal to the Council for a Directive extending the field of application of the reduced rate of capital duty from Continental style mergers to take-over operations in the British sense (EEC *Journal officiel* C 113, 28 October 1972).

[15] EEC Supplement to Bulletin No. 8—1967 of the EEC.

before the Council, deals with measures for adjusting direct taxes with a view to facilitating the development and interpenetration of the capital markets in the European Community[16].

On 16 January 1969, the Commission submitted to the Council two proposed Directives concerning:

(i) common taxation arrangements applicable to mergers, split-ups and the transfer of assets involving companies in different Member States[17]; and

(ii) common taxation arrangements applicable to parent and subsidiary companies in different Member States[18].

Questions of corporate taxation and capital movements were examined in a Commission Memorandum on the Community's industrial policy, submitted to the Council on 18 March 1970[19].

On 30 June 1970 the Commission submitted to the Council the Proposal for a regulation on the creation of a new company form, the 'European Company'[20]. The tax rules are mainly those of the two draft Directives of 16 January 1969, mentioned above.

So far, no concrete Council decision has been taken in the field of direct tax harmonization. Apart from the Memoranda just referred to, only the two proposed Directives (on mergers and parent company/subsidiary taxation) will be outlined.

(*a*) *Cross-frontier Mergers*

There are three problems to be solved;

The first one is the taxation of the so-called 'hidden reserves', an element of the true value of an enterprise not yet taken into account by the respective national tax administration. When two national companies merge, the national tax administration may disregard this higher value, because none of the merging companies leaves the country. A cross-frontier merger is considered as dissolution of the absorbed company involving liquidation and, therefore, taxation of all true values not yet taxed. This means that companies merging across frontiers are

16 EEC Doc/COM(69) 201 of 5 March 1969; see also *Bulletin of the European Communities*, May 1969, pp. 22–23.
17 EEC *Journal officiel* C 39, 22 March 1969.
18 EEC *Journal officiel* C 39, 22 March 1969.
19 EEC Doc/COM/C 70/100 fin. of 18 March 1970.
20 See Supplement to Bulletin no. 8—1970 of the EEC.

at a disadvantage compared with companies merging at national level.

The second problem is the fact that the country which loses one of the merging companies also loses a taxpayer.

The third problem is the taxation of establishments of the merging companies in third countries.

In the Community, neither the company laws nor the tax laws of the various Member States provide scope for cross-frontier mergers. Nor are there any tax rules, since tax provisions follow company law provisions, and these do not exist. Once company law has been extended to cover cross-frontier mergers, tax barriers must also be eliminated. In its draft Directive the Commission proposed common tax arrangements for cross-frontier mergers.

As regards the first of these problems, the Commission sees the solution in a system under which the taxation of the assets not yet taxed is deferred until they are converted into cash. To avoid abuses, these assets must be registered in the books of the merged company before the cross-frontier operation is completed. No tax should be levied at the time of merger. Where the second problem is concerned, the state which loses the taxpayer should keep the right to tax the establishments of the merged company which remain within its territory.

The third problem cannot be solved by extending the existing conventions on the avoidance of double taxation. The system of these conventions is incomplete. The practical solution of these conventions generally consists in the states concerned renouncing the right to tax these establishments. It seems necessary to centralize the taxation of these third country establishments in the state where the new company has its registered office, and to allow this company to deduct from its taxable profits the losses of these establishments. But this presupposes the harmonization of corporation taxes to avoid tax havens.

As an immediate solution the Commission proposes that the State where the company has its registered office should waive its right to tax the profits of these establishments except where the company opts for the so-called 'world profits' system. Under this system, all profits are taxed in the state where the registered office is located, with allowance being made for profits already taxed in the states of the establishments. To avoid abuses, the system must be applied to all establishments in the EEC for a period of at least five years. The companies should have the right to limit this 'world profits' system to certain third countries so as to diminish the risk involved.

(*b*) *Taxation of Parent Companies and Subsidiaries*

The Commission proposed the elimination of all double taxation of dividends distributed by subsidiaries to their parent companies in different Member States. The profits which the parent company receives from its subsidiaries should be exempt from corporation tax in the hands of the parent company. Furthermore, no withholding tax at the level of the subsidiary company should be withheld.

Finally, parent companies which have very substantial holdings (at least 50 per cent in their subsidiaries may opt for the system of consolidated profits). Such a system would enable the parent company to set off the losses made by any subsidiaries against profits made by other subsidiaries.

In its Programme for the Harmonization of Direct Taxes of 26 June 1967, the Commission proposed as long-term objectives in the field of corporation taxes and personal income taxes:

(i) a general tax on company profits, having the same structure throughout the Community and based on broadly similar methods of assessment and rates;

(ii) a single comprehensive personal income tax which admittedly may differ from one member country to the other for a long time to come.

According to the Resolution of 22 March 1971 concerning the establishment of economic and monetary union, the Council should—in the first three-year-phase—decide on measures concerning:

(i) the harmonization of certain types of tax which might have a direct effect on capital movements within the Community, and in particular the harmonization of the tax system applicable to interest on fixed-interest securities and to dividends;

(ii) further harmonization of the structure of company taxation.

Three subjects from this list of short-term measures are of immediate interest:

(i) harmonization of the rates of withholding taxes on interest on bonds;

(ii) harmonization of the rates of withholding taxes on dividends;

(iii) a common system of taxing undistributed as opposed to distributed corporate profits.

These three matters are closely interrelated, but once the third problem is solved, the other two may be solved more easily, so we shall concentrate on the third problem, sometimes referred to as the economic double taxation of dividends.

At present, three corporation tax systems are in force within the Community. Germany applies the two-tier (or 'split rate') system, charging a reduced rate of corporation tax on distributed profits. France and Belgium, on the other hand, are applying the imputation system; they grant the relief within the scope of the personal income tax by allowing the shareholder a 'tax credit', that is to say, allowing him to deduct from his personal income tax liability part of the corporation tax paid by the company distributing the dividends.

The other Member States, i.e. the Netherlands, Luxembourg and, from 1 January 1974, Italy, have made no arrangements to avoid this double taxation. These countries apply, just as at present in the UK, what we now call the classical system. Under this system, a partial relief can be given by means of lowering the uniform rate of the corporation tax.

On a comparison of the different systems, an exhaustive study has been carried out for the Commission by Professor Van den Tempel of the University of Amsterdam, till recently Chairman of the Fiscal Committee of OECD[21].

Professor Van den Tempel came to the following conclusion in respect of a common system for the EEC: 'If the domestic and the international aspects of the systems are reviewed together, the conclusion seems to be justified that system A (the classical system) is the most suitable to be adopted as a harmonised system in the European Communities.'

It will not be easy for the Commission to propose a common

---

[21] EEC No. 15/1970 of the series 'Competition; approximation of legislation'.

system. As is well known, there are not only economic and technical problems, but also political and even philosophical differences of opinion behind the phrase 'economic double taxation of dividends'.

At least, by now, the issue lies only between the classical system and the imputation system.

Spontaneous Harmonization in the Community

As has been stressed recently by the Director-General for the Internal Market and Approximation of Laws, M. Vogelaar, much harmonization is in progress in addition to the formal processes of Commission Draft Directives, Council Decisions, etc. Fiscal reforms in each Member State often tend towards a common norm, and indeed, sometimes these common moves are the initiating factor in formal processes of harmonization.

For example, in recently discussing impending German fiscal reforms, a senior official of the German Ministry of Finance listed four principles governing such reforms: simplicity, equity, maintenance of revenues, and conformity in the EEC. In Italy, the current consolidation of imposts on companies into a corporation tax is, in a way, the adoption of a Community system. In other cases, e.g. the introduction of the French beer excise in 1969, a confrontation between national plans and Commission thinking has produced modifications in those plans.

The interdependence of national reform plans and Commission proposals for harmonization is very understandable, when it is remembered that the process of consultation between members of national ministries and members of the Commission may continue for several years before the stage of publication of a Commission draft directive is reached.

Of course, in the case of the corporation tax, this is one area where national reform plans and the Commission's studies have not led in the same direction. The UK is following France and Belgium in having an imputation system. Thus, there is certainly a latent harmonization between several Member States, but the latent harmonization is not necessarily in the same direction as the Commission's philosophy. However, the tendencies towards conformity in the Member States are by no means complete. There is a difference between the formerly proposed German and UK imputation systems. German proposals involve complete crediting, the UK only partial[22]. More significant, the Netherlands, Luxembourg, and from the 1 January 1974, Italy, have a classical system, and it can be argued that technically the Belgian system is a modified classical system rather than an imputation system. Among the new members, the UK is familiar with the classical system, and Denmark has a modified form of it[23].

In general, therefore, there has been much spontaneous harmonization among Member States, and in accord with Commission thinking, in the field of indirect taxation, VAT and excises, and only corporation tax seems to remain outside of this interdependent process of national reforms and Community harmonization.

Tax Harmonization and Enlargement of the Community

Let us consider the situation regarding harmonization from the point of view of the three new Member States. The Treaty of Accession was signed on 22 January 1972. The Treaty contains a large number of Articles, Annexes and Protocols, as well as an exchange of letters on monetary matters, and some of these Articles, Protocols, etc., relate to fiscal harmonization. Let us look at the principal references.

Article 38 regulates the progressive elimination of customs duties of a fiscal nature. The new Member States can, however, replace the fiscal element in such duties by internal taxes under the terms of Article 95 of the Treaty of Rome. When this is difficult, the Commission can permit the continuance of such customs duties until 1 January 1976. It has been foreseen in a supplementary report that such a situation exists with tobacco imports into the UK; these import duties can be continued if the harmonized structure of tobacco excises is not fully in force by 1 January 1976. Article 138 gives Denmark the opportunity to opt out, until 30 June 1974, of the provision of Article 95 as it relates to table wines.

Annexes I, VII, and XI contain further fiscal provisions.

---

[22] Today it is, however, quite uncertain whether the new Coalition Government of the Federal Republic will keep to the plans for an introduction of an imputation system.

[23] Analysed in EEC *Journal officiel*, 27 March 1972.

Annex I enumerates the adaptations mentioned in Article 29 of the Treaty of Accession, to acts adopted by the institutions of the Community. In that which deals with fiscal matters, only small text adjustments are foreseen in connection with the Council Directive of 17 July 1969 governing indirect taxation on the raising of capital.

In Annex VII, based on Article 133 of the Treaty of Accession, two fiscal directives are mentioned. In the case of the first, the Directive of 28 May 1969 concerning duty-free allowances for cross-frontier travellers, Denmark is given, until 31 December 1975, the right to exclude manufactured tobacco, certain alcoholic drinks, and beer, from exemption from sales and excise taxes. Secondly, in connection with the Council Directive of 17 July 1969, concerning indirect taxes on the raising of capital, the UK and Ireland are allowed, in certain circumstances, not to apply some of the provisions which came into effect on 1 January 1973 on the fiscal treatment of mergers and takeovers.

Article 152 of the Treaty of Accession states that all directives and decisions applying at the moment of joining, 1 January 1973, must be applied in the new Member States, except where specific provision for delay is stated. Specific delay, mostly for six months, has been allowed in Annex XI in the case of the following directives:

Application of First and Second Directives on VAT (Directives of 14 April 1967): for UK, until 1 July 1973; for Ireland, until 1 January 1974.

Application of Third Directive on VAT (8 December 1969): for UK, until 1 July 1973.

Application of the Directive of 17 July 1969 on indirect taxation on the raising of capital: for Denmark, until 1 July 1973.

It is worth noting that all the legal acts of the Community up to 10 November 1971, some 3,000, have been examined in meetings between the Commission and delegations of the candidate states. And from that time, all new propositions of the Commission to the Council have been communicated to the candidate states and consultations on them have taken place.

The process of the new Member States conforming to the fiscal harmonization already achieved by the Six appears fairly easy in the case of the introduction of the system of VAT.

Denmark, since 1967, and Ireland, since November 1972, already have such a system, the UK will introduce it on 1 April 1973. Similarly, the extension to the Nine of the measures in process of achievement by the Six concerning travellers duty-free allowances, and indirect taxes on the raising of capital, should not be difficult.

It is true that future measures of fiscal harmonization may be more difficult to achieve on the basis of accord between nine members compared with six. But latent or spontaneous harmonization, discussed earlier, is going to play a big part in easing the way. For example, change is in the air in several of the new members concerning VAT, corporation tax, social security and personal income tax.

Of course, acute points of difficulty are going to arise. Some examples from the field of indirect taxation are:

(i) the issue of zero VAT rates on food in the UK;
(ii) the number of VAT rates in Denmark;
(iii) level of VAT in Ireland;
(vi) level of excises in all three new members.

These, and many other fiscal problems must be solved eventually, sometimes by new members conceding to the Community position. But, on the other hand, with the new Member States playing a full part in consultations and decision-making, the Community position will often itself be strongly influenced by the arguments of one or more of the new Member States.

7

Future Tax Policy of the UK as a Member of the EEC

by Douglas Dosser

The New Significance of Tax Harmonization

DISCUSSION of British taxation and the functions of the budget must be fundamentally affected by British entry into the Community: every tax and budgetary move will have to be viewed in relation to the Community harmonized tax system and the European budget. Policy itself will be impelled along certain directions of fiscal changes which at least in part will be determined by Britain acting in accord with Community decisions. So it is particularly vital at the present moment to define an economically sensible Community tax harmonization programme, in the hope that British negotiators will use their substantial influence in that direction.

In this final chapter, we endeavour to suggest what a sensible tax harmonization programme would consist of. Some of the suggestions fly in the face of the tendencies already established by the Commission. But this is precisely the moment to evaluate and, where necessary, challenge those directions. Although it implies long-range perspectives in taxation, rather than the next budget, now is the time when fundamental directions will be established.

The general tenor, or philosophy, of the chapter is to pursue certain gains in the field of taxation and public expenditure which may be achieved by British entry, but to preserve a certain national fiscal flexibility and avoid the 'harmonization mania' of which the Commission has sometimes been accused.

Fiscal Harmonization and Economic and Monetary Union

As emphasized in chapter 1, the subject of tax harmonization now has to be seen as one plank among several in the construction of economic and monetary union. This change of emphasis is particularly important. For it may fairly be argued that some at least of the present tax harmonization tendencies in the Community are too Neumarkian and pre-Wernerian; that taxation as a plank of economic and monetary union implies new directions.

With the advent of the goal of economic and monetary union, the issue between equalization and fiscal flexibility, as discussed in chapter 1, is joined more acutely than ever before but, we suggest, with considerably more weight to the fiscal management school. Necessity for the economic management of the whole European economy, and its parts, is enhanced at the very time that the range of tools is diminished, for example, by the eventual elimination of exchange rate variation between Member States, as monetary union is achieved. In this situation, fiscal flexibility becomes an imperative.

In a wider, post-Wernerian framework, it is not just taxes that must be considered from the point of view of economic management; tax harmonization has to be increasingly viewed as part of the growth of the European budgetary system.

Just as we have got used to considering the allocative, stabilization, distributional roles of the national budget, and to considering tax and public expenditure measures in relation to all three aspects, now we must consider the Community fiscal system in the same three aspects of the European budget.

At the same time as we emphasize the importance of fiscal flexibility, certain arguments for a unified European tax system have to be acknowledged. An integrated system is a symbol and engine of European integration, and the finance of the growing European budget by taxation demands a certain uniformization.

The position sought therefore must be a compromise between the requirement of fiscal flexibility for modern economic management, and uniformization for European economic integration and Community finance.

The Constraints on Fiscal Harmonization

The endeavour to reconcile these two rather opposed goals, of fiscal flexibility and fiscal uniformity, has to be made in the context of a variety of constraints, administrative, political and economic.

In mentioning some that seem relevant and important, they do appear to have a common theme—the difficulty of extreme or rapid change towards economic and monetary union envisaged by Wernerism. This being so, some might wish to argue that they are only temporary, whilst others will consider them to be permanent constraints if they are seeking a looser European federation than Werner implies.

(*i*) *Administrative Constraints*

We should recall more clearly than we usually do in this field the extremely diverse tax systems in the nine members of the Community for which tax harmonization is beginning. In many cases, the historical tax system is closely related to deep national, cultural and religious characteristics. Thus some tax changes are going to be costly and difficult.

It is the area of personal taxation, compared with what might loosely be called business taxation, where the difficulties are greatest, especially so in the case of the Personal Income Tax and the Social Security systems. These should be excluded from present consideration for immediate harmonization, since to harmonize personal allowances and various welfare systems is to cause the maximum affront to cultural characteristics with the minimum of economic gain. Similar considerations apply on the expenditure side of the nation's accounts. For example, business-type expenditures such as those on transport might be harmonized later on, whilst welfare expenditures such as those relating to national health services will prove much more difficult to harmonize and less worthwhile.

Even when the case for the harmonization of business taxes has been clearly made, the costs and difficulties are usually underestimated. To give a couple of examples, the administrative extension of the VAT to the retail stage in Italy, with reasonable coverage, is going to take many years to achieve, and again the costs of the private sector of the introduction of VAT in Britain have been grossly underestimated on the official side.

(ii) Political Constraints

Of course, in a sense, the whole paper could fall under this heading since the degree of tax harmonization achieved over the next ten years will be a function of the political interplay of the nine Member States. However, we mean to stress just one great political aspect at this juncture, and that is the balance that the Member States will want to achieve in, say, the next ten to fifteen years between the transference of fiscal sovereignty.

Of course, this is once again the issue between, on the one hand, the Unification School (as represented by Wernerism, and by the Brussels Commission), and on the other hand, the Federalist School.

The fundamental political assumption in this is that the Federalists will hold most sway during the ten to fifteen year period roughly considered, especially in view of the contemporary British political situation, which will lead to Britain's influence largely pushing in this direction.

The fiscal implication is that large areas of national fiscal sovereignty will be maintained as far as one can see in the future. Wernerism is little appreciated in Britain.

(iii) Economic Constraints

Whilst the economic gains from tax harmonization are the main point of this chapter, it is as well to point out here that constraints also arise from the economic side. For example, the adoption of a Community system for a particular tax which involved a substantial regressive effect on the distribution of income in one country or another, or a serious deterioriation in the balance of payments, is going to vitiate against the popularity and progress of the whole Community idea in that country.

It does not necessarily mean that where a Community system scores well on a number of political and economic grounds, but has one bad economic aspect, that it must necessarily be abandoned. We should think instead in terms of compensatory fiscal measures, which might lie entirely within the remaining national financial sphere.

The Implied Community Tax System

We now want to suggest a system which divides fiscal

sovereignty between the Community and the Member States, strikes a compromise between the call for European fiscal integration and the need for national fiscal sovereignty, leaves room for fiscal management of the economy, and keeps as close as possible within the constraints discussed.

We urge consideration of this system as a basis for considering what would be best for Britain in the Community, and sensible in economics for the Community itself.

The system is founded mainly on broad political and economic precepts—it is a grand strategy. It has more important secondary consequences on domestic British economic factors such as the cost of living, unemployment, etc. Evaluation of these consequences forms a task to keep Government and academic economists busy for a long while once more detailed specification of this (or some other system) becomes available. What few detailed hypotheses have become available have been analysed in previous chapters, e.g. the value-added tax chapter. These are sparse at present, and new analyses of new hypotheses are much to be desired.

The first task is to make a proper distinction between the Community tax system and Member State tax systems. The first division is between those taxes which, following our previous principles, should be Community taxes, wholly or in part. Our list of the corporation tax, the value-added tax, and excise duties is consistent within the current plans of the Community. Conversely, Member State taxes, the personal income tax and social security levies and receipts should remain Member State taxes.

Where a Community tax is concerned, the need for harmonization of the structure is clear. It is often expressed as a need for transparency, but the real point is that contributions to the European budget can only be equitable between Member States when the base upon which those contributions are levied is an identical one in each Member State.

This immediately implies structural harmonization of the corporation tax, VAT and excises. This is again consistent with the present Commission's aims. However, the levying of an equal rate of tax in each of these three fields, and its eventual transfer in the long-term to finance the Community budget is not implied at all, and quite undesirable. All that is needed, given structural harmonization of these three taxes, is an equal rate sufficient to provide a focus of economic integration for the Community as a whole, sufficient to finance the growing European budget, and necessary where the allocation of resources would otherwise be misdirected in an undesirable way.

These principles are satisfied by the following: corporation tax should be levied at an equal rate throughout the Community and form the basis of European budgetary finance; the VAT should be composed of a certain equal percentage rate levied in each Member State on behalf of the Community, and possibly the same for excise duties.

A variable percentage rate, of VAT and of excises, should be levied in each Member State, and the proceeds remain with that Member State. These national and variable parts of the VAT and excise duties form the area of taxation, together with the personal income tax and social security contributions, which remains within the fiscal discretion of the nation state.

This system meets the following fundamental principles as broadly as is possible:

(i) There is scope for those concerned with integration and unification, since the structures of the three Community taxes have to be harmonized, and an equal rate established for the whole of the corporation tax, and segments of the VAT and excises. Ample revenue is, furthermore, provided for a sizeable European budget

(ii) Considerable scope is left for national diversity in tax systems. The personal income tax and social security system can remain strongly reflecting national attitudes towards welfare benefits, their size and nature, and ample revenue is forthcoming for the welfare budget of each Member State, from these two taxes and from the variable part of the VAT and excises. Each Member State can choose the level of its welfare state through its own domestic taxes, including variation of the discretionary part of the VAT.

(iii) The misallocation of resources due to differential taxation within the Community, which has always exercised the Community's tax harmonizers so much, is minimized. Trade in products is little affected provided the destination principle remains in force, since imports and the home-produced article will each pay the Community rate and the national discretionary rate of VAT or excise duty. As regards factors of production, the system is consistent with the fact that capital is entirely mobile, and labour likely to remain very immobile. Therefore, any differences in the corporation tax, such as national discretionary rates on top of a Community rate, would, especially with the growth of the multi-national corporation, immediately distort the location of production. Tax differences in respect of workers, such as the differences in personal income taxation, will not have the same effect.

(iv) Fiscal flexibility is retained, in the discretionary parts of the Community VAT and excise duty, and in the rates of Member State taxes. National variations in these, perhaps in consultation with other members of the Community, can therefore be used for stabilization policies of Member States, bearing in mind the new difficulties of adjusting one Member State in relation to the others once exchange rate variations are eliminated.

(v) The costs of change are minimized. For example, it is much easier to get companies on same tax system than individuals.

This proposed system contravenes the present Commission plans, official and unofficial, in the following respects:

(1) Whilst at present VAT is the leading candidate for tax harmonization, eventually it will be only partially a Community harmonized tax. It is the corporation tax which is to take up the running, and progress on harmonization of the corporation tax is much more urgent than on VAT and excises.

(2) The destination principle has to remain in force for the VAT and excises.

(3) Instead of the eventual aim of equalization, or a narrow band, of rates for the VAT and presumably in the long-run for the corporation tax and excises, the goal needs to be complete equalization for corporation tax, but wide bands of national discretion, over and above a small basic Community rate, for VAT and excise rates.

As a brief illustration of how the scheme would look in Britain, we could paint the following picture. A corporation tax would be levied on all corporate enterprises in Britain whether British-owned or owned by companies registered in other Member States. This may be levied at a rate of 40 per cent or less. This revenue is passed over to the Community budget. Whether a withholding at a common rate would still be necessary is a debatable point, but probably not, as all proceeds are going to be passed to the Community budget anyway. When dividends are received by a national in any Member State from a corporation in any Member State, these are taxed under the national's personal income tax system. If the present British system of separation of corporation tax and the personal income tax were maintained as the Community system, as strongly recommended by the Commission's own Tempel Report, there are no major complications. If, however, the Member States (including Britain) are going to demand an alleviation of the so-called 'double taxation of dividends' by a variation of the French credit method, as now recommended by the Select Committee on the corporation tax, then a decision is necessary as to whether the Member State or Community is going to suffer the reduction in revenues that results. The complications are not insurmountable, but the simplicity of the Tempel system is all the more to be commended.

In the case of the VAT, the tax base, including definitions and exemptions, would be harmonized in the same way as the corporation tax. But only a small percentage beginning with the 1 per cent of 1978 (1975 for the present Six) and rising to perhaps 2 per cent or 3 per cent is levied on behalf of the Community and passed over to the European budget. The remaining percentage, over say 3 per cent, which might range from as little as 7 per cent to 17 per cent, is the national discretionary rate. A similar bi-partite system might be applied to the major excise duties, or they could remain national discretionary taxes.

The personal income tax and social security systems will remain much the same, although they may need a little adjustment to take account of the mobility of executive manpower, and to meet the argument that the social security contributions of firms are equivalent to the corporation tax.

A rough idea of the division of tax revenue between the Community budget and the British budget which this system would imply can be obtained as follows. Using National Income

Blue Book statistics for 1970, some £2,300 million would go to the European budget out of a grand total of tax revenues of £14,700 million. This figure for the payments to the European budget is obtained by summing the receipts of the corporation tax and one-third of the combined receipts of the purchase tax and selective employment tax (since a 10 per cent value-added tax roughly covers the combined revenue of these taxes, and above we postulated a 3 per cent Community rate).

This compares with a projected White Paper contribution by the UK to the European budget of some £500 million by 1980. But this sum is for the support of agriculture alone, and no allowance is made for the expansion of the other policies which it is expected will emerge beyond 1980.

The order of magnitude of tax revenues to be paid to the European budget which the proposed system implies may seem rather high. It does seem to imply that the floating card, excise duties, should be left in the area of national taxation. Alternatively, the payments to the central budget can be lowered by a reduction in the Community rate under the VAT.

The Expenditure Side of the European and Member State Budgets

We have spent most of the time on the division of tax revenues between the European budget and the Member States. A similar division will have to be made between the expenditure side of the central and national budgets.

At present, agricultural support accounts for 86 per cent of the European budget. With the accession of new members less interested in agricultural problems, this must quickly be supplanted or supplemented, by support policies for particular types of industry, for regional development, and for joint assistance to Associate Members and other less-developed countries.

Using the well-known conceptual classification of budgetary functions as between allocation, redistribution and stabilization, it would appear that the main functions of the European budget should be to influence the allocation of resources into particular industries and regions.

The redistributive function of the Euro-budget will be confined to inter-state redistribution. The joint foreign aid programmes are of course of this nature. But also, in the longer run, there is no reason why an element of progressivity in tax and expenditure programmes should not be introduced into the Community to the benefit of poorer areas, since such a principle applies to inter-person redistribution in each of the Member States.

The Community will meet two kinds of stabilization problems, the adjustment of the whole Community and its balance of payments to the outside world, and adjustments between one Member State and another. If we assume that in future the Community has a common currency, exchange rate differences between Member States are eliminated. Thus the tool of exchange rate variation remains for Community/Rest-of-World adjustment, making little demand on Community fiscal adjustment (which could nevertheless be made through the Community taxes). But between Member States the absence of exchange rates and balances of payment puts more weight on the need for adjustment through fiscal means. It is suggested that a distinction has to be made between short-run and longer-run Member State stabilization. Longer-run stabilization policy lies in the hands of the Community budget. This comes about through structural improvement in a sector or region. Thus the support policies must have a growth aspect (support for new-technology industries) and a stabilization aspect (the reviving of stagnant industries and/or regions).

When we come to the Member State budgets, a difference of emphasis might emerge. In the foreseeable future, a good deal of the allocation role, including support policies for particular industries and regions, is bound to continue. But in the long run, the Member State budgets may concentrate much more on the equity or social welfare side, rather than on economic efficiency.

Just as we made a distinction between so-called business taxes, such as the corporation tax, and national taxes with strong cultural content, such as the personal income tax, it is going to be much easier to centralize business-type expenditures, and thus cause less affront to national cultures, than to try to uniformize or transfer sovereignty over, say, national health services, family allowances systems, and the degree of redistribution of income that a Member State desires for itself.

The redistribution side of the Member State budget is therefore about transfers between persons or income groups, whereas the limited redistributional aspect of the Community budget revolves about certain inter-State transfers.

In the stabilization branch of policy, the Member State budget must continue to have considerable play, whether through expenditures on goods or transfers between individuals. This is because of the absence of other equilibrating methods. Our system allows the variation of the national tax and expenditure system to help manage the demand aspects of the economy in the short run, through, for example, the discretionary rates of VAT and personal income tax. The long run adjustment of a constituent economy or large part of it cannot be achieved in this way, since the downward or upward movement of taxes and expenditures have their limits; variation of the exchange rate to overcome this problem has to be reached by structural support policies of the European budget.

Concluding Remarks on the British Position

The UK should press for the corporation tax as the main part of the Community tax system, for the reasons which have been given earlier in this chapter. Unfortunately, the Community has already set off down the less desirable road of making the VAT the Community tax. The best corporation tax for the Community to use would be that recommended by the European Commission's Tempel Report, which coincides with the present British system.

The European budget so financed should concentrate on economic functions, not social welfare ones, with perhaps some attention to inter-state transfers. The UK should insist on the permanent retention of a large area of fiscal sovereignty. The personal income tax and social security systems should remain national systems, and a large part of the VAT and excise duties should also fall under national discretion.

The national budget so financed should take care of the social welfare aspirations of each Member State, and provide for the inter-personal distribution and internal stabilization roles that the modern budget now performs in Western economies.

With such a division of taxation and budgetary functions accepted, the UK should be willing to foster the progress of

Community harmonization of company law and agreed tax fields, so that the Community is, for its part, operating a true budgetary role in the same way that, for their part in the system, the Member States are.

The Process of Fiscal and Budgetary Development

What has been said—concerning the functioning of the European budget and its financing—might be accepted as a goal, but the road toward it seen as a daunting one.

For example, the obvious objection to the idea of the use of the corporation tax as the main instrument of Community lies in the present heterogeneity of corporate law and practice between one Member State and another. This is, of course, a serious problem, which would lead to great inequity in the national and sectoral distribution of the Community tax burden. However, it should be remembered that the harmonization of corporate law is just as much an objective of Community development as harmonization in the harmonizable tax areas.

The unification of corporate law *and* the corporate tax base could therefore be seen as a single process. The way ahead appears to be in the creation of a European company code, under which some companies in some Member States would incorporate. It could be these companies which paid tax on their earnings to the Community. This would provide a gradual transition from national corporation taxes to a European one, and a gradual build-up of Community budgeting revenues.

Two problems arise: for the first, companies may require an incentive to incorporate under European tax law. Since they are likely to be multi-national companies, the advantage of a streamlined tax payment on a multiple Member State operation might be sufficient. Alternatively, some slight tax advantage compared with the total to be paid to Member State administration might be necessary as an interim measure.

The second problem is that, during this transitional phase, inter-Member State equity as regards contributions to the Community budget is unacceptable, depending as it would on the proportion of a Member State's business which was transacted by European companies. An equalization scheme would be necessary in the transitional period, and a balance struck between Member State contributions on the basis of total corporate earnings in each state or some other measure of business activity.

If these difficulties of transition can be overcome, an important advantage is added to the previous merits of the corporation tax as the main Community fiscal instrument: namely, that the development of European company law and taxation becomes a single, mutually-reinforcing, programme.

So much for the transitional problems of reaching a suggested goal of Community financing. Similar transitional problems are involved in moving toward the goal of a Community budget with an extended business-oriented expenditure programme.

In this connection, the issue is over the development of proper Community budgetary principles, and an abandonment of the narrow outlook of juste retour.

A low-quality budgetary expansion would occur thus. Regional problems, or unemployment, reaches crisis proportions in some parts of the Community. At a Heads of State Summit meeting, a plan of subsidization is hammered out, with reference to 'who-gets-what' from this and existing settlements. That is to say, the regional or unemployment problem is dealt with in a way corresponding to the determination of the Common Agricultural Policy. When the principles, with juste retour well to the front, are settled at the Summit meeting, the Commission executes them through the European budget. In this case, the budget is merely a book-keeping implementation of the principles politically agreed elsewhere.

A departure from this scenario would involve confining a Summit meeting to the broadest of principles, and allowing Community institutions more discretionary powers to implement a regional or employment policy. The policy would then be implemented by reference to Community welfare, and may involve a departure from juste retour. Probably, a redistributional aspect would then creep into the Euro-budget, just as it is usual for national budgets to assist ailing regions or industrial sectors to an amount exceeding their financial contributions to the budget.

As this situation can be realized—the operation of Community principles of disbursement of funds, involving, where necessary, the partial abandonment of juste retour—so the Euro-budget becomes a budget with similar instrumental powers as those of a national budget in Member States' economics.

This may be a longish process. We have defined the goal, in terms of financing and expenditures for expansions of the European budget, but the process toward it involves a strengthening of Community law and institutions.

APPENDIX

EEC Decisions, Regulations, Directives, etc., Relating to Taxation

(As at 1 February 1973)

General

I. Own Resources

Decision 70/243
Decision of 21 April 1970 on the replacement of financial contributions from Member States by the Communities' own resources. (O.J. No. L 94 of 28.4.1970.)

Regulation 2/71
Regulation of 2 January 1971 implementing the Decision of 21 April 1970 on the replacement of financial contributions from Member States by the Communities' own resources. (O.J. No. L 3 of 5.1.1971.)

II. Economic and monetary union

Resolution of the Council and of the Representatives of the Governments of the Member States of 22 March 1971 on the phased introduction of a Community Economic and Monetary Union. (O.J. No. C 28 of 27.3.1971.)

Resolution of the Council and of the Representatives of the Governments of the Member States of 21 March 1972 on the application of the Resolution of 22 March 1971 on the phased introduction of a Community Economic and Monetary Union. (O.J. No. C 38 of 18.4.1972.)

Direct Taxes

I. Proposals for directives and regulations

A. Tax arrangements for mergers, scission and contribution of assets. Tax arrangements for parent and subsidiary companies

1. Proposal of 16 January 1969 for a Council Directive on the common tax arrangements applicable to mergers, scission and contribution of assets involving companies in different Member States. (O.J. No. C 39 of 22.3.1969.)

2. Proposal of 16 January 1969 for a Council Directive on the common tax arrangements applicable to parent and subsidiary companies in different Member States. (O.J. No. C 39 of 22.3.1969.)

B. European company and joint undertaking

1. Proposal of 30 June 1970 for a Council Regulation embodying a statute for European Companies. (O.J. No. C 124 of 10.10.1970.)

2. Proposal of 29 July 1971 for a Council Regulation on the application of the statute for joint undertakings to activities in the hydrocarbons industry. (O.J. No. C 106 of 23.10.1971.)

3. Proposal of 17 September 1971 for a Council Regulation on the creation of joint undertakings within the scope of the EEC Treaty. (O.J. No. C 107 of 25.10.1971.)

II. In preparation

A. Structure of corporation tax and withholding taxes

Preliminary drafts of directives on the harmonization:
— of corporation tax structures
— of withholding taxes on dividends
— of withholding taxes on interest from bonds

B. European Cooperation Group

Preliminary draft of a directive on the establishment of a European Cooperation Group

Indirect Taxes

A. VAT

I. Directives

1. *Directive* 68/221/EEC
Directive of 30 April 1968 on a common method for calculating the average rates provided for in Article 97 of the Treaty. (O.J. No. L 115 of 18.5.1968.)

2. *Directive* 67/227/*EEC*
First Directive of 11 April 1967 on the harmonization of legislation of Member States concerning turnover taxes. (O.J. No. 71 of 14.4.1967.)

3. *Directive* 67/228/*EEC*
Second Directive of 11 April 1967 on the harmonization of legislation of Member States concerning turnover taxes—Structure and procedures for application of the common system of value-added tax. (O.J. No. 71 of 14.4.1967.)

4. *Directive* 69/463/*EEC*
Third Directive of 9 December 1969 on the harmonization of legislation of Member States concerning turnover taxes—Introduction of value-added tax in Member States. (O.J. No. L 320 of 20.12.1969.)

5. *Directive* 71/401/*EEC*
Fourth Directive of 20 December 1971 on the harmonization of legislation of Member States concerning turnover taxes—Introduction of value-added tax in Italy. (O.J. No. L 283 of 24.12.1971.)

6. *Directive* 72/250/*EEC*
Fifth Directive of 4 July 1972 on the harmonization of legislation of Member States concerning turnover taxes—Introduction of value-added tax in Italy. (O.J. No. L 162 of 18.7.1972.)

II. Proposal of 26 *February* 1968 *for a Council Directive* on harmonization of the laws of Member States concerning turnover tax—Common detailed rules for the application of value-added tax to operations relating to agricultural products (will be incorporated in the draft directive under III). (O.J. No. C 48 of 16.5.1968.)

III. In Preparation
Draft directive on the common value-added tax system: uniform assessment.

B. Excise duties

I. Directives
Directive of 19 December 1972 on taxes, other then turnover taxes, imposed on the consumption of manufactured tobacco. (O.J. No. 000 of 00.0.0000.)

II. Proposals for directives and decisions
1. Proposal of 28 December 1970 for a Council Directive on the harmonization of specific consumption taxes on liquid hydrocarbons for use as combustible fuels. (O.J. No. C 14 of 11.2.1971.)
2. Proposals of 7 March 1972 for directives on excise duties and similar taxes. (O.J. No. C 43 of 29.4.1972.)
(a) Proposal for a Council Directive on excise duties and indirect taxation, other than VAT, imposed directly or indirectly on the consumption of products (outline proposal);
(b) Proposal for a Council Directive on the harmonization of excise duties on alcohol;
(c) Proposal for a Council Directive on the harmonization of excise duties on wine;
(d) Proposal for a Council Directive on the harmonization of excise duties on beer;

(e) Proposal for a Council Directive on the system of excise duties to be applied to mixed drinks.

3. Proposal of 7 March 1972 for a Council Decision setting up an 'Excise committee'. (O.J. No. C 43 of 29.4.1972.)

III. In preparation

Proposal for a Council Directive on the harmonization of excise duties on mineral oils.

C. Duty-free allowances in international travel

I. Directives

1. *Directive* 69/169/*EEC*

Directive of 28 May 1969 on the harmonization of provisions laid down by law, regulation or administrative action relating to exemption from turnover tax and excise duty on imports in international travel. (O.J. No. L 133 of 4.6.1969.)

2. *Directive* 72/230/*EEC*

Second Council Directive of 12 June 1972 on the harmonization of provisions laid down by law, regulation or administrative action relating to the rules governing turnover tax and excise duty applicable in international travel. (O.J. No. L 139 of 17.6.1972.)

II. Proposals for directives

Proposal of 22 September 1972 for a third Council Directive on harmonization of the laws, regulations and administrative provisions concerning turnover taxes and excise duties applicable to travellers;

and

Proposal of 22 September 1972 for a Council Directive on duty-free allowances as regards imports of goods sent in small packages to private persons. (O.J. No. C 113 of 28.10.1972.)

D. Capital duty

I. Directives

1. *Directive* 69/335/*EEC*
Directive of 17 July 1969 concerning indirect taxes on the raising of capital. (O.J. No. L 249 of 3.10.1969.)
2. *Adoption*, on 6 December 1971, *subject to consultation* with the new Member States, of the proposal (O.J. No. C 34 of 14 April 1971) for a Council Directive fixing common rates of capital duty.

II. Proposal of 21 September 1972 for a *Council Directive* extending the field of application of the reduced rates of capital duty. (O.J. No. C 113 of 28.10.1972.)

E. Dealings in securities

In preparation

Proposal for a Council Directive on the harmonization of indirect taxation on dealings in securities.

F. Insurance

In preparation

Proposal for a Council Directive on the harmonization of indirect taxation on insurance contracts.

G. Transport

Proposals for a directive and a decision

1. Proposal of 17 July 1968 for a first Council Directive on the reorganization of national systems of taxation on commercial vehicles. (O.J. No. C 95 of 21.9.1968.)

2. Proposal of 29 March 1971 for a Council Decision on a common system of tariffs for the use of transport infrastructures. (O.J. No. C 62 of 22.6.1971.)

Index

Index